SAMCHOONOGL

TEACHERS

COMMUNITY
AUTONOMY and
IDEOLOGY in
TEACHERS' WORK

AMONG SCHOOL TEACHERS

COMMUNITY AUTONOMY and IDEOLOGY in TEACHERS' WORK

Joel Westheimer

FOREWORD BY LARRY CUBAN

TEACHERS COLLEGE
COLUMBIA UNIVERSITY
NEW YORK AND LONDON

Published by Teachers College Press, 1234 Amsterdam Avenue, New York, NY 10027

Library of Congress Cataloging-in-Publication Data

Westheimer, Joel.
   Among schoolteachers : community, autonomy, and ideology in
teachers' work / Joel Westheimer ; foreword by Larry Cuban.
     p.   cm.
   Includes bibliographical references (p.) and index.
   ISBN 0-8077-3745-3 (cloth : alk. paper). — ISBN 0-8077-3744-5
(paper : alk. paper)
    1. Teaching—Social aspects—United States—Case studies.
2. Teachers—Social networks—United States—Case studies.
3. Interpersonal relations—United States—Case studies.   4. School
management and organization—United States—Case studies.
5. Education change—United States—Case studies.   I. Title.
LB1775.2.W37   1998
371.1'06—dc21   98-12184

ISBN 0-8077-3744-5 (paper)
ISBN 0-8077-3745-3 (cloth)

Printed on acid-free paper
Manufactured in the United States of America

05   04   03   02   01   00   99   98   8   7   6   5   4   3   2   1

To my parents,
who put education above all else and
who encouraged me to follow my heart
at every step and every choice. They taught
me the importance of community.

Contents

Foreword

C ALLS FOR DEVELOPING teacher communities within America's schools as a major tool to revitalize teaching and learning are well over a decade old. Initially growing out of a major reform surge in the mid-1980s to involve teachers in schoolwide decision making, practitioners, policymakers, and researchers have seen in teacher collaboration a seedbed for school reform. The appeal of transforming the workplace to make it more professional while making it personal and communal have brought disparate school reformers together in head-nodding agreement that teacher communities will renovate the landscape of traditional schooling.

Like so many other ventures in the history of school reform, the allure of building and sustaining teacher communities in schools is magnetic—at first glance. After all, how could one be so obtuse as to argue against the logic or, for that matter, the inherent obviousness of groups of teachers collectively helping students learn more and better? As in so many other appealing reforms, however, fundamental questions go either unasked or are neglected by their respected yet unvarnished cheerleaders. Exactly what are teacher communities? What are they after? How do they begin? Do they evolve through stages? How alike or different are they from one another? How are such communities built?

It is to these important questions about the anatomy of a compelling yet largely unexamined school reform that Joel Westheimer turns in this engaging account of two such teacher communities. In describing and analyzing the three-year-old teacher communities in the Louis Brandeis and C. Wright Mills Middle Schools, Westheimer finds no evolutionary phases through which these professional communities climbed. In these two settings where teachers work together closely he finds substantial differences in ideology that rippled outward into personal and professional relationships, how the curriculum was managed, and how classroom and school discipline were handled. With much fine-grained detail about how each professional community conducted its daily affairs, Westheimer dips beneath the surface glamour of teacher communities to reveal key commonalities but, to my mind, more importantly, the sharp differences between the two.

Both are clearly instances of professional communities but each is founded on different beliefs and behaves in ways unlike the other. The structures within the two communities that are essential to their existence are identified and analyzed sufficiently to conclude that there are different types of teacher communities. In this analysis, Westheimer leaves in tatters the tapestry of rhetoric that has been woven by reformers around the idea that all teacher communities are alike and that building them requires only a few hardy souls with moxie and determination.

What gives heft to this account of two exemplary professional communities is how the author anchors the study in the theoretical literature on community and how he conducted the study. In grounding his analysis of the idea of community in the work of both philosophers and social scientists such as Tönnies, Dewey, Selznick, and Bellah he identifies those generic concepts that apply to teacher communities within schools. Westheimer then places the aroused appeal for professional collaboration as a lever for reform in the mid-1980s in the aftermath of disappointment over state-driven school initiatives to overhaul public schools a few years earlier. The author ties together these two literatures to provide a context for the in-depth study of the Brandeis and Mills schools.

This is no once-over-lightly piece of research where the investigator spends maybe a week or two at the site and interviews key informants. Westheimer's inquiry spanned two school years. He interviewed dozens of teachers and administrators, observed teams as they worked through conflicts, attended most faculty meetings, sat in teacher lounges, and went to dinner with teachers. Drafts of what he wrote were shared with key informants and critiqued.

I make these points about the study and how it was done in two little-noticed West Coast schools to underscore what the author concludes about types of teacher communities, particularly about how teacher communities differ and the critical importance of ideology in shaping the mechanisms for building and sustaining community in each setting. Because of the conceptual underpinnings of the study and the meticulous care he invested in it, the implications of what Westheimer says carry far more weight with me than the assertions of oft-quoted champions for school reform that are founded on brief forays into the same schools cited over and over again in the research literature.

What makes this study compelling for me is the author's commitment to building teacher communities. A researcher's choice of subject is as much a matter of passion as anything else. And Westheimer believes deeply in the importance of community—his life, professional and personal, testifies to this value. Yet in doing this study, Westheimer displays also a passion for disciplined inquiry and an open-mindedness to reexamine his commitments. Where he ended up on the final page of this book was not where he started years earlier when he stepped into Mills and Brandeis. For these passions, for the quality of the study itself, and for the importance of teacher communities in school reform, Westheimer and Teachers College Press have done practitioners, policymakers, and researchers a considerable service in publishing *Among Schoolteachers*.

Larry Cuban
Stanford University

Acknowledgments

T HERE IS a certain irony in writing a book about community since so much of the work is done alone. I enjoyed the luxury of being able to reflect on themes of community without distraction, but solitude has its limitations. Not surprisingly, the most rewarding moments of this project did not come from isolated writing but rather from the many and varied exchanges with teachers, administrators, colleagues, friends, and family—the members of my own overlapping communities each of whom contributed a great deal to this project.

Larry Cuban has been an intellectual mentor like none other. Through his inseparable commitments to scholarship, schools, and the individuals who work within them, he is an inspiring model and colleague. I am deeply grateful. Nel Noddings' work on caring and community made the analysis set forth in this book richer. Lee Shulman's fine eye for inconsistency and his suggestion—along with Nel's—that I pay careful attention to the darker side of community made this study stronger.

Others contributed a great deal to this project. Mike Atkin, Milbrey McLaughlin, Ray McDermott, and David Tyack were always available for consultation. Betty Achinstein, Mimi Beretz, Michael Berkowitz, Lucy Bernholtz, Susan Christopher, Larry Glickman, Ellen Lagemann, Stephen Leckie, Gary Lichtenstein, Sonia Murrow, Judi Powell, Gordon Pradl, Marla Stone, Miriam Westheimer, and Jonathan Zimmerman gave thoughful feedback at critical moments.

Others who helped shape my ideas about teacher professional communities include: Sibyl Frankenburg, Amy Gerstein, Joan Kent, Catherine Lacey, Tom Meyer, Mike Pease, Bill Rice, and Jerry Rosiek. Ellie Moses and Fred Frank did the lion's share of transcribing interviews. Beverly Carter helped secure initial contacts with schools. I am also grateful to my research assistant at New York University, Bethany Rogers.

Emotional support came from friends and family: Michael Bader, Julie Duff, Joel Einleger, Susan Jackson, Erin O'Connell, and Lisa Petrides deserve special mention here. Eran Caspi and Danny Factor are old friends from Hashomer Hatzair, a youth movement that gave me experiences in community that I carry with me in virtually all my work as an educator.

I am especially grateful to two friends. Joe Kahne has been my intellectual ally. Not only is he responsible for much of the strength of the arguments in this book, but he could easily be blamed for the shortcomings. Pam Burdman read and re-read everything multiple times and was always available to keep me on track when I wandered.

The Spencer Foundation generously supported this research. I received additional support from the New York University School of Education's Griffiths Award and Research Challenge Fund. Also, parts of chapter 5 appear in an essay review I wrote in the *Harvard Educational Review* (vol. 66, no. 4, pp. 853–857).

Once this book landed at Teachers College Press, I was lucky to be placed in the hands of Susan Liddicoat and Karl Nyberg, both of whom made valuable contributions to the final manuscript. I am also grateful to Carole Saltz, Leyli Shayegan, Nancy Power, and Nina Spensley.

Above all, the teachers and administrators who agreed to participate in this study gave generously of their time and their wisdom. This book was made possible by their insights, their experiences, and their willingness to share their professional lives for more than a year.

I owe the completion of this book to Barbara Leckie who read draft after draft, providing thoughtful advice and constant support, and who believed in the importance of this work. She will always be my partner in travels of the mind as well as the heart.

Finally, since this book is about teachers, I should note the two most important teachers in my life. My mother and my father supported me in enormous ways and conveyed an irrepressible love of questions. During the final stages of writing this book, my father died unexpectedly. His quiet pride in my work, his strength of spirit, and his love stay with me.

AMONG SCHOOL TEACHERS

TEACHERS

COMMUNITY
AUTONOMY and
IDEOLOGY in
TEACHERS' WORK

Introduction

RECENTLY, I attended a series of lectures on the political history of the California city in which the fieldwork for this book took place. For the talk devoted to the McCarthy era, the organizers assembled a panel of individuals who had lived and been politically active in the city at the time. I remember one man in particular recalling a protest that he and another panelist had organized outside of a local meeting of the House Un-American Activities Committee (HUAC). He remembered a large, peaceful, and energetic gathering on the steps and outdoor corridors of the city hall and the sudden and unexpected emergence of police and firemen brandishing water cannons. The force of the water propelled people down the stairs, he explained. Then his eyes grew teary, and his voice faltered. His co-panelist got up from her chair and walked over to comfort him. She began to explain to the audience that these stories stirred memories of a very powerful time for them. It was only a few moments before she too began to cry. "Part of what makes me emotional," she said, "is coming here to tell you about a time when we felt so connected to one another, such a sense of purpose and meaning in our work, and how I don't feel that in my life today."

As often happens when one is deeply embedded in a scholarly project, the entire world seems to be speaking to the research. It was easy to leave this panel session thinking that the above incident was about community (and loss of community). After all, the co-panelists had been recounting their experience of connection, identity, and purpose through the meaningful work in which they were engaged. The discussion that followed that day seemed particularly relevant to my interest in teachers' work in schools: How, several in the audience wanted to know, were those working in opposition to HUAC able to accomplish so much despite enormous obstacles? How were they able to maintain high commitment to their work, to their beliefs, and to each other? Why is that kind of vocational engagement, dedication, and contentment so elusive? Indeed, I wondered, why do some groups of teachers in some schools seem able to accomplish so much and overcome enormous obstacles while maintaining their commitment to their work, to students, and to their colleagues while others do not?

1

One explanation, especially popular with the participants themselves, could be characterized by the well-known saying "being at the right place at the right time." Something about the individuals involved or the circumstance of their coming together may bring about unparalleled connections. Perhaps the frightening influence of HUAC in the mid-1950s was sufficiently compelling to inspire unusual commitment and a sense of responsibility. Similarly, perhaps schools with particularly compelling circumstances and a fortunate combination of the "right" teachers and administrators result in unusual richness and productivity. "We were very fortunate to have such amazing people here that year," a teacher might speculate. This happenstance explanation is the simplest and most common one given by teachers who have experienced the intensely engaging professional and personal connections familiar to some, but that are all too rare in most of today's schools. Not surprisingly, it is also the least satisfying explanation.

It is simple because it offers little more than the obvious: Good people in good places do good work. It is unsatisfying because it suggests that this type of good work, sense of place, and belonging is the result of a lucky alliance of committed individuals and arbitrary circumstance—hardly comforting to those who look toward policy and planned change to improve the educational climate of schools for students as well as teachers.

Educational policymakers, on the other hand, prefer a more hopeful explanation. Rather than assume arbitrary circumstance of people and place, reformers like Theodore Sizer, Roland Barth, Ann Lieberman, and many others have concentrated on changing the school as a workplace. As a result, advances have been made in moving teaching away from the "egg-crate" view of schools in which teachers are isolated in individual classrooms with virtually no opportunity for substantive contact with colleagues. Reformers have advocated new school structures that afford teachers time to meet and to plan interdisciplinary curriculum units. Some suggest smaller schools or dividing large ones into smaller schools-within-schools. Others focus on the professionalization of teaching, giving teachers greater authority and decision-making power. By focusing on the environment in which teachers do their work, these reformers hope to foster collegial work and interaction. Creating professional conditions more conducive to a sense of collective mission and responsibility has become an essential component of many local, state, and national school reform efforts (Barth, 1990; Hargreaves, 1994; Lieberman, 1995; Meier, 1995; Sizer, 1992).

The difference between the two explanations—a chance gathering of gifted individuals around an important issue versus the deliberate creation of organizational conditions that encourage communal ties—is more strategic than philosophical. We can all recall experiences in which we felt fortunate to be working with a particularly spirited colleague or group of colleagues on a compelling task. Many of my own experiences in schools and other educational settings make it tempting to search no further: I remember late-night planning sessions in the windowless storeroom of a New York City public school with two colleagues so deeply committed to their work and so adept at navigating around monumental obstacles that I simply thought I had been blessed with inexplicable good fortune; or the program-design group assembled to plan a one-week "immersion" unit on the presidential elections for which the planning time was easily three times the duration of the unit itself; and the work with Danny Factor, my co-director for an educational program in the San Bernadino Mountains with whom I continue to consult and exchange ideas. I felt lucky to have had such talented and committed colleagues.

Still, my sympathies lie with the reformers. I am convinced—and more so after completing this study—that there is much that can be done to foster conditions in schools that make teaching and learning vital, collegial, and socially as well as personally rewarding.

The complexity of this task, however, may have been greatly underestimated. Influential reports in the mid-1980s, such as *Tomorrow's Teachers* (Holmes Group Inc., 1986) and *A Nation Prepared* (Carnegie Task Force on Teaching as a Profession, 1986), spurred a series of reforms intended to enhance both teachers' and students' commitment to education by strengthening teacher and school communities. In fact, a broad and growing array of work focuses on the features of educational communities and their implications for policy and practice (Louis & Kruse, 1995; Merz & Furman, 1997; Raywid, 1993; Strike, 1991). Unfortunately, these reports and the growing bodies of research literature that bolster them were, and continue to be, disappointingly vague.

Several works demonstrate considerable insight into the practical and theoretical tributaries that those interested in building communities in schools must navigate (Louis & Kruse, 1995; Sergiovanni, 1994). These same works are less clear, however, when discussing the social and political forces that often turn tributaries into quagmires. Current descriptions do little to convey the serious challenges school personnel face in creating communities that reflect what John Gardner has called "wholeness incorporating diversity" (1991, p. 30).

There are many visions of community. Some seek to reinforce conservative notions of individual rights and freedoms while others pointedly question relations of power and authority. Some visions differ from one another in the convictions and motivations they represent, and some represent convictions and motivations that are alarming and dangerous. Before debating the proper course to steer toward stronger, more cohesive teacher communities, we must ask whether educators aspire to the same type of community. Policymakers, practitioners, and academics must question whether the widespread calls for community and shared commitment obscure the diversity of interests, ideologies, politics, and cultures represented in today's schools.

By relying primarily on theoretical scenarios or snapshot views of school and teacher communities, current works on community gloss over these essential and difficult questions. While education policymakers, for example, are quick to acknowledge the importance of developing shared beliefs in any community of practitioners, there have been virtually no studies that adequately investigate how these communities might accomplish such a fraught task. If teachers decide (as they did in one of the schools I studied) that the curriculum should be interdisciplinary and social-studies driven, how should the community accommodate a teacher who wants to teach math in a much more traditional way and with fewer links to other subjects? Or if teachers decide (as they did in Gerald Grant's [1988] *The World We Created at Hamilton High*) that teaching can and should be apolitical, should a teacher who is committed to having her students understand the forces that shape society through active political engagement be stopped? How can a school manage when one group of teachers would like parents to have a major influence in setting the educational mission of the school and choosing the textbooks while another group would prefer to contain the role parents play? These are the topics of real disputes in schools.

Similarly, surprisingly few works address the tough dilemmas that emerge when practitioners pursue the ideals of democratic, egalitarian communities, hoping to become neither excessively insular nor aimlessly diffuse. We frequently hear words like *tolerance*, *diversity*, and *multicultural perspective*. One can nod at the value of dissenting views, but without creating institutional structures that encourage and manage them, dissent is more likely to be suppressed or ignored than heard and considered. It is an important first step to advocate working together, overlooking differences, and creating friendlier, more open work settings; but it is an equally important second step to acknowledge insidious power imbalances and the resulting sense of impotence that threatens to undo so many reform efforts. Though numerous works on building community in schools make an eloquent case for teacher community, they fail to convey adequately the dilemmas that practitioners face. Nor do they suggest processes for overcoming them.

In this book, I explore the culture of two schools to uncover how the teachers and administrators in each have structured and negotiated their particular version of community. Specifically, I make explicit the beliefs that teachers share, the processes employed to balance and accommodate those that are not shared, and the ways that commonly held beliefs emerge from their collective experiences. Calls for a strong sense of community among teachers and students are ubiquitous, and few disagree with such a goal. But what these teacher communities would look like and how to move toward them are questions too often left to the imagination and frustration of those who work in schools.

Do teachers working together on lesson plans constitute teacher community? Are team-teaching, peer review, or schoolwide organizational changes likely to strengthen professional community? Neither the research literature nor reformers' plans adequately address these questions or the purpose, development, and maintenance of teacher professional communities. By favoring hypothetical scenarios over in-depth case studies, theoreticians obscure these tough issues and thereby evade the obligation of plodding through the muck, the ambiguity, and the mystery of how communities succeed and fail to manage conflict, ensure full participation by their members, and grow through overlap with other communities.

This book examines two schools that set out to change the way teachers go about their daily work. Influenced by the growing reform movement that aims to build community in schools, the teachers and administrators in these schools developed new organizational structures, taking notice of the school culture, specifically the nature of relationships and interactions among and between students and teachers. I began with two sets of questions, the first practical, the second theoretical:

1. *How* do actual teacher communities work? What structures and processes are in place to ensure participation by the weak as well as the strong, the shy as well as the bold? How are the inevitable tensions that emerge when people work together on substantive projects managed? What factors influence the growth of these teacher professional communities? What enduring problems and dilemmas impede them?
2. How might an in-depth observation of a community's day-to-day operation contribute to current theoretical understandings of community? How do these teacher professional communities support or challenge conceptions of community found in social theory, educational history and policy, and educational research?

In Chapter 1, I situate this book within the growing field of work that has already been conducted in educational research, social theory, history, and school reform, work that considers the relationships among teachers in schools. I highlight points that remain vague or ill-defined and that obscure important problems and possibilities for teacher professional communities in schools. I also discuss the appropriateness of the community metaphor and of academic discourse in describing relationships among teachers within a school or, indeed, relationships within any community.

Chapter 2 describes the efforts of faculty and staff at Louis Brandeis Middle School, one of two public middle schools in a suburban but demographically changing district. Once serving an overwhelmingly white, professional, middle-class population, Brandeis now boasts a student body that represents more than 25 countries and languages and a broad range of economic backgrounds. Founded originally as a junior high school, Brandeis has been undergoing structural reorganization in response to the growing national movement of middle schools.

In Chapter 3, I shift to C. Wright Mills Middle School, located in a large and ethnically diverse California city. In 1984, under a court-ordered consent decree agreement, Mills closed and reopened with a mostly new administration and teaching staff. Then, five years later, Mills underwent another series of restructuring efforts under California State Senate Bill 1274 (SB 1274), which provided small amounts of funding for schools to voluntarily restructure themselves.

Chapter 4 looks at the distinguishing features of the teacher professional communities in these two schools. By focusing on the differences and similarities in the types of working relationships and structures found in each community of teachers and by using grounded examples from each school, I reexamine common practical and theoretical understandings of teacher community. I argue that the mainstream reform rhetoric around teacher professional community is so broadly employed and dominant that it masks the enormous differences between these two schools.

In Chapter 5, I detail lessons learned from looking at these two schools. I highlight implications for teachers and administrators, and researchers and policymakers, and explore how these two schools might help to inform broader policy discussions on fostering teacher community in other schools. I also consider the implications for inquiries into democracy and community beyond the schools and the teaching profession.

Why should we care about teacher community in schools? "Today," writes John Gardner (1991), "we see a loss of a sense of identity and belonging, of opportunities for allegiance, for being needed and responding to need—and a corresponding rise in feelings of alienation, impotence, and anomie" (p. 7). Regretfully, schools too often reinforce the sense of detachment and passivity that Gardner observes. They confirm the assumption that someone else is in charge.

Recall the McCarthy-era political history panel I described earlier. The panelists recounted their work and their sense of association as if they were inseparable. Like those panelists, many young future engineers, health care workers, car manufacturers, authors, politicians, artists, lawyers, service providers, and countless others want to know that what they do matters, that they are connected to others, participating in feats of creation and making history. So do their teachers. Teaching and learning in their grandest sense are less about giving and receiving information than about what Maxine Greene (1988) calls "making lives." Teachers and schools can encourage students to see that there are reasons for the choices that we make, that these choices affect others, that they have the capacity to take part and to influence people and events, but teachers can accomplish such a task only if they believe it and experience it themselves.

One of the final questions asked of the panelists was this: "Did you stop the [HUAC] committee hearings?" It was posed by a 17-year-old woman ironically sporting a T-shirt that read "ASK ME IF I CARE" on the front and "I DON'T" on the back.

"Eventually, yes, I guess I would say we did," replied one of the panelists.

A guarded expression of awe appeared on the questioner's face. "I wish I had been there," she said softly.

CHAPTER 1

Community and Teachers' Work

> The idea of community is . . . elusive. There appears to be no clear consensus as to its central meaning.

S O WRITES Philip Selznick in his 1992 book, *The Moral Commonwealth: Social Theory and the Promise of Community* (p. 357). "It's my second favorite word," anthropologist Ray McDermott said to me of community (family is his favorite). "Every time someone uses it, I jump up. But when I'm working analytically, my use of it has a very high overlap with when I don't know what I'm talking about. As soon as I get confused, I pull out 'community'" (personal communication, 1993). Indeed, in 1955 noted biologist George Hillary found 94 different definitions of community. In choosing to use community as a metaphor and analytic term for examining teachers' work in schools, I place this book in precarious territory.

Social analysts have long found ambiguity in Americans' use of the term *community*. The anthropologist Herve Varenne (1986), for example, studying American conceptions of society and social diversity, concluded that there is tremendous confusion over notions of the individual and community. Comprising a strange amalgam in American usage, the words *individuality* and *community* are used at times to describe similar social arrangements and priorities almost interchangeably. Reconciling ideals of individualism and community while understanding their complexities has been an ongoing project for more than two centuries.

Ambiguity is not the only obstacle facing those seeking to use the term *community* analytically. Though much school reform literature tends to use teacher community in a universally positive way (meaningful relationships among teachers, a sense of collective responsibility for students and for each other), for many, community conjures up particularly negative visions: domination of the individual by the collectivity, religious communities insulated from the larger communities in which they are situated, stiflingly homogenous small towns or highly regimented cults. Many thinkers, writers, and policymakers question the prudence of pursuing community without careful attention to its darker side (Noddings, 1996; Selznick, 1992; Tillich, 1952). Furthermore, Americans' penchant for "rugged individualism" seems, to some, to conflict with calls for stronger communal associations. Some question whether idealized, liberal communities can exist at all—communities with a strong collective orientation that also maintain individual protections and freedoms (see Noddings, 1996).

Situated within this messy theoretical construct, then, this book carries with it some unintentional baggage: enormous variation and negative associations with the term *community*. So why use community to describe the social and professional bonds among teachers in schools and the circumstances, conditions, and contexts under which these bonds form and are maintained? Previous school research suggests that moving from a view of schools as formal organizations to one of schools as communities highlights "strategically different aspects of the school environment and fundamentally different levers for policy" (McLaughlin, 1993, p. 80; Sergiovanni, 1994). "The community metaphor," writes McLaughlin (1993), "draws [policy] attention to norms and beliefs of practice, collegial relations, shared goals, occasion for collaboration, problems of mutual support and mutual obligation" (p. 81). By attending to teacher professional communities, we gain an understanding of the ways in which teachers' relationships structure their work and their lives in schools.[1]

At the same time, by drawing on the sociological and philosophical literature on community, empirical work in schools can benefit from the progress that has been made in understanding communities—what they are, how they are formed, how they are maintained, and what causes their dissolution. This literature can help researchers to better understand the personal and professional relationships among teachers in a school setting. By contributing to the conceptualization of the community metaphor, its dilemmas, uncertainties, and shortcomings, this literature on community offers the possibility that the difficulties associated with its use may be outweighed by the benefits.

WHAT IS TEACHER COMMUNITY?

Many schools currently showcased by reformers share the characteristics that a growing number of researchers and practitioners consider essential: Teachers derive support, motivation, and direction from one another (Cohen, McLaughlin, & Talbert, 1993; Meier, 1995; Sizer, 1992). They

---

1. I use the terms *teacher professional community* and *teacher community* interchangeably to mean a community of teachers in school.

work collaboratively on curricular projects toward goals that they and their students find meaningful. Teachers meet during lunch, after school, and during preparatory periods to discuss curriculum, pedagogy, and individual students. These teachers are able to foster for their students and for themselves what John Dewey calls a "social" mode of learning. Rather than the isolation and professional alienation that seem so common in many of today's schools, these teachers experience a sense of membership. They are part of a community of teachers.

School districts across the country are implementing policies aimed at strengthening these professional ties among teachers, primarily through changes in school organization. Site-based management, magnet programs, and house systems, for example, group students and teachers in more intimate, self-contained, autonomous clusters. Reformers hope to see teachers work together within these structures as colleagues and professionals, ready to take responsibility for their own working environment as well as that of their students. Reflecting the work of sociologists, anthropologists, and political scientists who have long been interested in the ties that bind people together, reformers expect, as a result, that teachers will form communities that inspire their work and enrich the connections among themselves and their students (Barth, 1990; Darling-Hammond, 1988; Goodlad, 1984; Lieberman, 1988a; Smylie & Tuermer, 1995).

When reformers expect teachers to form professional communities, however, they imply that there exists an articulated and commonly understood notion of the type of community to which teachers should aspire. Consequently, they assume that, given the proper workplace conditions, teachers will know how to turn organizational potential into truly communal relationships; furthermore, they assume that teachers seek such communities. Voices from the field indicate otherwise.

In the schools where I have worked, as well as in those where I have observed, teachers and principals expressed an assortment of often contradictory beliefs about community. Some believed that professional community requires a sense of common mission; others pursued individual professional autonomy. Many teachers welcomed team-teaching and scheduling changes that allowed them to watch colleagues in the classroom; others preferred not to have their teaching observed. As recent studies have confirmed, teachers' understanding of their roles as professionals varies greatly (Feiman-Nemser & Floden, 1986; Hargreaves, 1990; McLaughlin, 1993; Merz & Furman, 1997; Metz, 1986; Smylie, 1992). Such findings help to explain the difficulties in pursuing teacher professional communities in schools. Current reforms that aim to build teacher professional communities do not adequately address these ambiguities, and may, in fact, encourage rather than reduce teacher isolation (Little, 1990).

If there is no clear consensus among practitioners on the meaning of teacher community, and if reform efforts may be based on erroneous assumptions, how, then, do we clarify what teacher professional communities might look like? With all that has been written on communities and their defining characteristics (for an overview, see Selznick, 1992), there is surprisingly little material that educational researchers can use for empirical work on school communities. Before delving into the specifics of the two schools described in this book, therefore, it is helpful to review previous inquiries that contribute to our understanding of community. To begin, I draw on the work of social theorists and educational researchers for guidance. These theorists' observations and insights (for example, Bellah, Masden, Sullivan, Swidler, & Tipton, 1985; Etzioni, 1993; Raywid, 1988; Sandel, 1982) help to sketch a preliminary picture of the features and qualities of communities.

THE THEORY AND PRACTICE OF COMMUNITY: AN OVERVIEW

Two primary areas of inquiry inform the exploration of teacher professional communities described in this book. First is the substantial body of conceptual literature devoted to understanding the hows and whys of various notions of community (Bellah et al., 1985; Dewey, 1900/1956, 1916; Gardner, 1991; Selznick, 1992). Drawing on their own experiences, social theory, and political philosophy, these authors paint broad analytical portraits of their visions of healthy communities. These writings have a lengthy history including the work of the ancient Greek philosophers.

A second body of work on teacher leadership, collegiality, and school restructuring emerged in the mid-1980s, spurred by a series of influential reports. Documents such as *Tomorrow's Teachers* (Holmes Group Inc., 1986), *A Nation Prepared: Teachers for the 21st Century* (Carnegie Task Force, 1986) and *What's Next? More Leverage for Teachers* (Education Commission of the States, 1986) generated what Zeichner (1991) and others have called a "second wave" of educational reform. Unlike earlier reports, *A Nation at Risk* (National Commission on Excellence in Education, 1983) for example, this literature focused attention on teachers' professional culture, their empowerment, and the school contexts within which teachers spend their day (Barth, 1990; Hannaway & Talbert, 1993; Lieberman, 1986, 1988a; McLaughlin, Talbert, & Bascia, 1990; Wittrock, 1986).[2]

---

2. While these reports redirected the reform focus and discourse, many expressed concern over their immense claims and "mystifying innocence" about school change. See, for example, Apple (1987) and Cuban (1987).

As one might expect, the conceptual literature on community is not always applicable to schools. Moreover, the work that does address school communities focuses primarily on students and the importance of nurturing in them a sense of purpose and affiliation (Newmann & Oliver, 1967; Raywid, 1988). Though many reformers assert a connection between teacher community and school community (Barth, 1988; Lieberman, 1988b; Meier, 1995; Shulman, 1989), notions of teacher community have received little scrutiny. On the other hand, school restructuring literature, which honors teachers as central players, alludes to teacher community frequently while rarely attempting to conceptualize it with any rigor.

Why combine these two areas of inquiry? Those formulating theoretical conceptions of community can learn from the work of practitioners struggling to bring teachers together; similarly, practitioners benefit from greater reflection on the assumptions and, at times, competing visions that teachers, administrators, and policymakers carry with them as they begin to reshape their workplace habits and conditions.

In the following I explore different works on community, focusing on generalized but coherent notions that contribute to an understanding of school-based teacher professional community. My claim is that the absence of empirical research in the school workplace that distinguishes between different conceptions of teacher professional community has led both researchers and practitioners to overlook significant individual and organizational factors contributing to the survival or dissolution of these communities. If we make these distinctions clearer, the paths to creating and maintaining teacher professional communities in schools become easier to follow and the obstacles easier to avoid.

The Views of Social Theorists

Central features of community, according to contemporary theorists, include interaction and participation, interdependence, shared interests and beliefs, concern for individual and minority views, and meaningful relationships. The anticipated effects on individuals who belong to such communities include a sense of identity and belonging, affirmation, commitment to the group, strong bonds, and the development of both common purposes and collective responsibility.

Interaction and Participation. A community without interaction and participation among its members, social analysts agree, is a contradiction. "A flourishing community has high levels of participation," Selznick (1992) asserts. "People are appropriately present and expected to be present, on many different occasions and in many different roles and aspects" (p. 364).

It is through association and interaction, psychologists note, that human beings satisfy their need for attachment and social bonds (Bronfenbrenner, 1979; Erikson, 1963; Fromm, 1941). Similarly, sociologists and political scientists emphasize the sense of identity and the commitment that result from participation in community. Voting, speaking in public meetings, tutoring, and inculcating a sense of community responsibility in children enlist individuals in the collective quest for mutual engagement and commitment (Barber, 1984; Etzioni, 1993; Gardner, 1991). Human experience, notes Dewey (1938), is inherently social and, therefore, depends on interpersonal contact and communication within community.

It is noteworthy that Dewey and others also assert the converse to be true: Interaction and participation depend on experience (Dewey, 1916, 1938; Gardner, 1991). Described often as indicators *of* community, experiences that foster interaction and participation are also seen as requisites *for* community. In other words, community may be a side effect of continued interaction and participation directed toward other goals. The resulting sense of community also enriches and facilitates future interactions (Dewey, 1938; Greely, 1975). The reader may be aware at this point of the seemingly loose distinction theorists make between features, conditions, and processes of community. I discuss this uncertainty later in this chapter.

Interdependence. In *Habits of the Heart* (1985) Bellah and his co-authors define community, in part, as "a group of people who are socially interdependent, who participate together in discussion and decision-making, (see above) and who share certain practices that both define the community and are nurtured by it" (p. 333). Interdependence and shared practices that foster reciprocity and mutual need are cited often as essential components of community (Raywid, 1988; Scherer, 1972; Selznick, 1992). If members of a community do not need each other, the bonds between them become strained or contrived. Conversely, social theorists argue, when individuals are mutually dependent, they form attachments and commitments to the community as a whole (Hirschi, 1969).

Interdependence among community members should not be confused, however, with what Bellah calls "communities of interest" (Bellah et al., 1985). Examples of the latter include singles bars, investment pools, and the more recent condominium-owners boards. Each of these relies on interdependence among members and each could conceivably become what theorists reviewed here would agree is a rich community. Based solely on individual pursuits and gains, however, these examples of conjoining self-interests may do little to foster a common identity and sense of commitment. For reciprocity to be sufficient, writes Selznick (1992), "mutuality cannot be very narrowly focused. It must go beyond impersonal exchange, beyond coordination for limited goals" (p. 362).

Shared Interests and Beliefs. Most theorists agree that community must be built on a foundation of shared understandings. "Certain essentials are required in any community," writes Scherer (1972). These include "a 'core of commonness' or communality that includes a collective perspective, agreed-upon definitions, and some agreement about values" (pp. 122–123). Similarly, Selznick (1992) argues that the bonds of community are strongest when they rely on "shared history and culture" (p. 361). These can derive from a common language, ideology, or purpose and can be developed by projects that engage members of the community in the kinds of meaningful interactions described above.

The early Israeli kibbutzim serve as fine examples of Scherer's (1972) core of commonness. These collective agricultural settlements were generally founded by a group of members who shared a commitment to an egalitarian life-style within a social democracy. Kibbutz members shared a common heritage and culture, and common political convictions and ideals (Bettelheim, 1969; Blasi, 1978). Though there were significant differences among individuals, these early pioneers came with and paid a great deal of attention to forging a common *Ha'Shkofat Ha'Olam* (world outlook). Other examples of groups with a core of commonness include the founders of Jane Addams' Hull House, Mothers Against Drunk Driving (MADD), and various activist organizations with specific missions and beliefs.

Shared beliefs and common values characterize many communities that may or may not satisfy the other attributes listed here. Many theorists point out the dangers of communities based solely on shared beliefs (Bellah et al., 1985; Noddings, 1996; Raywid, 1988). While cults such as that led by the infamous Jim Jones or, more recently, David Koresh's Branch Davidians clearly boast collective beliefs, few would call them healthy communities. The press for conformity in communities has been pointed to again and again as an unresolved danger in both philosophical and practical discourse (Hoffer, 1951; Nisbet, 1953; Peshkin, 1986; Selznick, 1992).

In the extreme, one need venture no further than the growing popularity of neofascist groups to recognize the hazard of beliefs that are shared without question. Deciding which beliefs are "worthy" and which are not, however, is a thorny enterprise. This is illustrated in recent debates over a multicultural curriculum. Whose ideas are worthy? Whose beliefs should be shared? (see Taylor, 1992).

The challenge of communal association, theorists assert, is to foster a cohesive set of beliefs and interests while recognizing and growing from a plurality of ideas and perspectives. This brings us to the fourth feature of community identified by contemporary analysts.

Concern for Individual and Minority Views. Members of a community, while sharing interests and a commitment to one another, don't always agree. Individual differences, theorists argue, are not only inevitable but also foster growth within the community (Gardner, 1991; Greene, 1985; Selznick, 1992; Walzer, 1983). The capacity for critical reflection, therefore, is essential (Newmann & Oliver, 1967). Ideally, communities provide forums for exchange that lead to growth as new perspectives are considered. When consensus cannot be reached, compromise often permits communities to remain cohesive while acknowledging the diversity of members (Gardner, 1991).

Pluralism, these theorists assert, depends on a system that allows diversity while maintaining a level of coherence. Gardner (1991) explains that

> the common good is first of all preservation of a system in which all kinds of people can—within the law—pursue their various visions. . . . The play of conflicting interests in a framework of shared purposes is the drama of a free society. (p. 15)

Such ideas date back at least to the pluralist doctrines of Aristotle (who conveniently excluded women and slaves from his considerations of a good society) and are found in writings from de Tocqueville to Dewey and beyond. In the 1950s, for example, the sociologist Robert Nisbet (1953) emphasized the importance of embracing diversity while engaging in what he called "the quest for community." More recently, philosophers have challenged hegemonic (dominant) notions of value and worth in an effort to "de-marginalize" those traditionally left out of community discourse (hooks, 1994; Rabinow, 1984; West, 1990).

Arguments for diversity within community are often confused with arguments for individual rights, justice, and tolerance—those put forth by Rawls (1971), for example. The confusion stems from the idea that individual freedoms are in conflict with strong collective community beliefs. For this reason, many would be critical of the type of community found in fundamentalist schools such as the one described by Alan Peshkin in *God's Choice* (1986), in which a dominant set of beliefs curbs individual choices and beliefs. It is important to note, however, that those seeking to characterize the intrinsic strengths of community life do not narrowly view the protection of divergent views as a safeguard against "domination of the collectivity." These theorists reject the liberal dichotomy of individual freedoms versus the needs of the collectivity. Instead, they see diversity of ideas as an integral and desirable means for the growth of the community and of its individual members (Bellah et al., 1985; Dewey, 1916). First, these theorists suggest that embracing minority viewpoints promotes progress and enables communities to adapt to the demands and exigencies of a changing world (Gardner, 1991). Second, rather than being submerged within the group, individuals and their interests flourish specifically through their participation in the community (Dewey, 1916).

Meaningful Relationships. Included in the social theory of community is a relatively small body of work that sets out to clarify the meaning of community as it relates to schooling. These writers warn that children and adults currently have little or no sense of affiliation and identity and, in an effort to ameliorate these conditions, urge schools to undertake deliberate efforts to become communities. Schools, they argue, must provide a sense of connection and purpose since traditional sources for connectedness have broken down (Gardner, 1991; Raywid, 1988; Strike, 1991; Wehlage, Rutter, Smith, Lesko, & Fernandez, 1988).

Some educational theorists focus on schools' unique position as sites for community-building—places where students and teachers spend much time. Their vision of community in schools is sensitive to, but does not necessarily stem from, concern over weakening bonds outside the school. Rather, they hope to improve the quality and recast the priorities of schooling by making schools vibrant and transformative communities that both reflect and reexamine the larger outside community (Dewey, 1900/1956; Greene, 1985).

The vision of school communities that emerges from this literature is consistent with the four features of community described above. These theorists believe, for example, that those who spend much of their lives in schools should share commitments to interaction and participation (Raywid, 1988, 1995) and that schools should seek to provide children and adults with a sense of interdependence and shared beliefs (Grant, 1988; Newmann & Oliver, 1967; Power, Higgins, & Kohlberg, 1989; Rosenholtz, 1989). Particularly, however, they are concerned about a fifth feature of community: relationships.

Since schools are often characterized as alienating and isolating institutions, these theorists highlight the social nature of interactions within school communities. As Goodlad writes in *A Place Called School* (1984, p. 92), "The most important thing about school for the children and youth who go there is the living out of their daily personal and social lives." John Dewey (1916), for example, believed that school should be "a form of social life, a miniature community" in which each individual refers "his own action to that of others, and [considers] the action of others to give point and direction to his own" (pp. 87, 360). Dewey recognizes the potential inherent in the profoundly social interrelationships within schools to provide both students and teachers with continuity of experience, unity of learning, and interaction and affiliation. When school organization and curricula stray from these understandings, he notes, they are at risk of becoming detached and irrelevant at best, and miseducative at worst (Dewey, 1938).

Similarly, Nel Noddings (1988) envisions a pedagogical ethic that would emphasize individuals and groups caring for one another. Drawing on a rich body of feminist research on moral education, Noddings (1988, 1992) argues that school organization, curriculum development, and teaching practices should all be developed with an eye toward both children's and teachers' relational development. Her suggestions for curriculum design and implementation make clear and concrete commitments to interaction and participation within relationships. The inherently relational basis for school communities is a common emphasis among many writers (Bowman, 1984; Bruffee, 1987; Coleman, Hoffer, & Kilgore, 1982; Gardner, 1991).

Common Features of Community: A Summary

The constitutive features of community, according to social theorists, include the following:

1. *Interaction and participation.* People have many opportunities and reasons to come together in deliberation, association, and action.
2. *Interdependence.* These associations and actions both promote and depend on mutual needs and commitments.
3. *Shared interests and beliefs.* People share perspectives, values, understandings, and commitment to common purposes.
4. *Concern for individual and minority views.* Individual differences are embraced through critical reflection and mechanisms for dissent and lead to growth through the new perspectives they foster.
5. *Meaningful relationships.* Interactions reflect a commitment to caring, sustaining relationships.

Having mapped the features of community most commonly invoked by those who study and seek to build community among teachers in schools, I now turn to some issues these features raise.

PROBLEMS IN CONSTRUCTING A THEORY OF COMMUNITY

I have already noted some of the difficulties encountered when using *community* as a metaphor and analytic tool for studying schools (vagueness of the term and negative associations with the concept). At this point, I want the reader to be aware of two additional problems with the features of community that I described.

Characterizing Community Using Academic Discourse

The five features of community identified by social theorists do not render an entirely satisfying definition of community to those who have experienced the strong ties these features seek to describe. Do these features or characteristics constitute a way to identify communities, a checklist to assure ourselves and others that a particular alliance of individuals is or is not a community? To say yes would be to construe community as a static entity—one that an analyst could examine in a snapshot and know in its entirety. Few social analysts would be comfortable with such a simplification. Dewey and others see community as an ongoing series of interactions and experiences rather than a static state. They see it as a process. In Chapters 2 and 3, vignettes from two schools I studied provide a window into understanding the nature of this process. While the features I have outlined provide a common language for recognizing communities and their constitutive elements, they do not define community. Nor, I imagine, would they convince others of its importance. Used in conjunction with vignettes and ethnographic analysis, however, they contribute a great deal to the construction of a coherent framework for understanding communities in practice.

What is community like? Why is it important? These are perhaps the most difficult questions to answer through the use of conceptual literature, though many have tried. Reading about community, like reading about love, falls short of the experience. Nonetheless, the presence of community has indications and consequences on which many theorists agree. It is these indications and consequences that we can loosely call features. These features provide a common vocabulary for researchers examining communities in practice.

Distinguishing Between Features *of* and Processes *to* Community

A second, related ambiguity plagues discussions of community: Can we separate "features of" and "processes to" community? Not always. The traditional barn-raising may help to clarify this point. Local residents work together to build a neighbor's barn. This event is often seen as testimony to the strength of 19th-century rural communities. While barn-raising clearly requires strong bonds among neighbors, it is also a community-building experience. As local families engage in a common effort, their interdependence is made clear and their connections to one another are strengthened.

Similarly, school reformers view teacher professional community as a desirable outcome of restructuring plans. Specifically, they might seek, for example, to increase interaction and participation among teachers. Community, however, both shapes and is shaped by interaction and participation. If the outcome is itself a process (and community may well be an ongoing process), then what we have been calling the "features" of community may themselves be both "features of" and "processes to" community. As will become clearer in the following section, current reforms rarely differentiate between organizational conditions and community-building processes.

REFORM EFFORTS TO BUILD TEACHER PROFESSIONAL COMMUNITIES

The literature on school restructuring that aims to build teacher professional communities focuses on four overlapping approaches.

1. *Smaller schools.* By designing smaller, more intimate schools (often called "personalization") or segmenting existing schools into smaller, independent programs ("school-within-a-school"), reformers hope that teachers will interact more, participate more in designing curriculum and running the school, and develop a greater sense of connection and commitment (McLaughlin, Talbert, Kahne, & Powell, 1990; Meier, 1989, 1995; Ratzki, 1988).

2. *Magnet programs.* By coupling schools with a particular theme or educational focus, reformers hope that teachers will self-select schools with philosophies and beliefs similar to their own and be drawn together through the development of common beliefs and understandings (Meier, 1989; Metz, 1986; Raywid, 1984).

3. *Site-based management.* By giving teachers greater decision-making control over their workplace (also called "teacher empowerment"), reformers expect that teachers will increase participation in and commitment to the community (Barth, 1990; Cuban, 1984; Goodlad, 1990; Lieberman, 1987; Sizer, 1992).

4. *Collegiality and collaboration.* By encouraging teachers to share ideas, discuss teaching strategies, and work together in planning, teaching, and advising (related strategies include "team-teaching," "peer coaching," "action research"), reformers hope to reduce teacher

isolation and facilitate stronger professional connections (Lampert, 1991; Lieberman, 1988a, 1995; McLaughlin, 1993; Shulman, 1989).

Ambiguity in Reformers' Conceptions of Teacher Community

The visions of teacher professional community implicit in the reform literature described above are numerous and diverse. Though Hillary's (1955) paper detailing 94 definitions of community predates most of this literature by three decades or so, there is little material here in this generation of reformers and researchers that clarifies or reconciles ambiguous (and sometimes contradictory) visions of teacher professional community. There remains, in the literature specifically concerned with practice and policy, tremendous variation.

Barth (1988), for example, envisions "school as a community of leaders" (p. 640). Rosenholtz (1989) sorted the schools she studied into those that were collaborative and those that were isolated. Lieberman (1988c) writes: "The more that teachers share leadership, responsibility, and accountability with one another and with their principals, the more they come to perceive the school as a community" (p. 6). Metz (1986) reports conflicting conceptions of professional relationships in urban magnet schools. All allude to unspecified conceptions of teacher professional communities.

This latitude, which in theory may contribute to new ideas, in practice leads to uncertainty and ambiguity in policy decisions. Although there is some recent research that demonstrates the importance of professional community for teachers (McLaughlin, 1993; McLaughlin & Talbert, 1993), reformers rarely characterize the nature of such communities, focusing instead on the conditions necessary for their growth. As McLaughlin and Talbert's Center for Research on the Contexts of Secondary-School Teaching has found, work on the subject to date "has not yet been able to identify and investigate the dimensions which constitute [teacher] professional community or to discover how each of these dimensions works to support or undermine teaching" (Perry, 1997, p. 37; Little & McLaughlin, 1993).

In a professional culture plagued by "endemic uncertainties" (Lortie, 1975) and scarcity of time, resources, and status (Johnson, 1990) and a national culture characterized by independence and individuality (Bellah et al., 1985; Tocqueville, 1848/1966), reform efforts that provide only vague conceptions of teacher professional community are easily thwarted. In "Persistence of Privacy: Autonomy and Initiative in Teachers' Professional Relations," Judith Warren Little (1990) reports that the most common configurations of teacher-to-teacher interaction may do more to bolster isolation than to diminish it; the culture that Lortie described as individualistic, present-oriented, and conservative is thus not altered but is indeed perpetuated by the most prevalent examples of teacher collaboration or exchange. (p. 511)

Feiman-Nemser and Floden (1986) report similar disparity. The "cellular" nature of teaching in schools, they found, may be seen either as an unfortunate lack of mutual support or as a welcome guarantee of professional autonomy (p. 517). Management plans that grant teachers greater decision-making authority often free teachers from bureaucracy but do not connect them to one another. As one teacher said in a workshop on enhancing teacher collegiality,

Planning the science/writing fair [an attempt to bring together students and teachers from different disciplines] was a nice opportunity to work with all of you, but it's done little to make me feel that we're all moving in the same direction or that I should care a lot about what goes on outside my classroom. (1992 workshop notes, p. 4)

As a result of ambiguity in conceptions of teacher professional community, implementation of reforms aimed at fostering teacher community are received with a mix of confusion, mild concern, and doubt (Rosenholtz, 1989; Smylie, 1992).

Reform Assumptions

Popular leadership strategies such as site-based management, house systems, and magnet programs aim to build teacher professional communities by creating smaller, more personal settings and by granting teachers greater control over their school. These are organizational adjustments: changes in the arrangement, conditions, and hierarchies under which teachers work. As I noted earlier, when reformers expect these changes in the organization and leadership of the school to result in strong teacher professional communities, they assume that (1) teachers and administrators know how to turn organizational potential into truly communal relationships and (2) teachers seek such communities. Though there may be such schools, the studies cited above as well as my own experience in schools suggest that teachers may neither know how nor seek out ways to develop these communities. Some teachers enjoy watching their colleagues teach and having their colleagues watch them; others prefer to be left alone. In some schools, teachers meet frequently to design school policies and to work together on semester-long interdisciplinary projects; in many schools, teachers shy away from collective undertakings.

How might these assumptions limit our understanding of the formation and maintenance of teacher professional communities in schools? In making these assumptions, we do not distinguish between organizational conditions and processes of community-building. Smaller schools may provide conditions that make the establishment of teacher professional communities a possibility, but they do not necessarily engender the support, sense of shared mission, and strong personal ties that social theorists say are hallmarks of healthy communities.

The traditional norms of schools often constrain the development of communities. There is a long history of individuality, an emphasis on autonomy, and competition in schools and in society. Connecting teachers to one another may require more than setting the conditions for those who embrace community to have the opportunity to participate. It may, for example, require enacting experiences and processes designed specifically to build teacher professional communities (Westheimer & Kahne, 1993).

Schools, moreover, are frequently subject to teacher turnover. Therefore, sustaining a community from year to year demands an institutional culture and set of practices capable of regenerating community. This is no easy task. Institutional history and resistance to change demand that those pursuing community do more than hope that new teachers will work well with seasoned veterans. Community is not self-winding.

Organizational conditions, then, may be necessary but are not sufficient. "The educator," writes Dewey (1938), "is responsible for [selecting activities] which lend themselves to social organization, an organization in which all individuals have an opportunity to contribute something" (p. 56). The same could be said of reformers (or administrators, or teacher educators). What is important here is that the assumption that, given proper conditions, community will "happen" may be an erroneous one. Conditions are one thing, processes are another, especially processes that acknowledge individual and organizational factors as they influence outcomes of community-building.

Current organizational reforms may "empower" teachers, but they will not necessarily foster strong bonds in hierarchical and isolating school environments in which teachers value control of their own classroom and must often compete for scarce resources, prestige, and choice assignments (Bacharach, Bamberger, Conley, & Bauer, 1990; Bacharach, Bauer, & Shedd, 1986; Conley, 1991). A strictly organizational view of reforms that seek to build teacher professional community, then, obscures significant cultural factors that facilitate or block the formation of teacher professional communities. What approach, then, can be used to broaden the exploration of teacher professional communities beyond the study of organizational conditions? I take up this question in the next section.

THE STUDY

Of approximately 100,000 schools, governed by 75,000 school board members, employing some 2½ million teachers across North America, I observed only two.

When researchers observe any event, they are, in effect, shining a spotlight on their area of inquiry and simultaneously darkening all others. The circle of light that is cast both illuminates the interior and eclipses all that falls outside. Whenever we engage in revealing certain aspects of an event, we must recognize that we are likewise concealing other aspects of the same event. This is, on reflection, necessary in order to avoid the influx of an unworkable mass of information. As adults, we learn to select from an infinite supply of stimuli to make sense of our world. Research, however, in its most restrictive form, often fails to accommodate a sufficient diversity in ways of viewing or revealing. How, then, do we ensure a variety in our selection of data? We must encourage different ways of seeing, and of knowing (Goodman, 1978).

The dog in Gary Larson's cartoon (see Figure 1.1) has a selective view very different from that of the humans. Unaware of the nuclear war that is transpiring, the dog is concerned only with the fact that there appears to be another dog nearby. The dog is shining his spotlight on a different place.

All the events in the cartoon may be considered "fact." Nonetheless, to propose that there is one way of knowing and framing these facts is to deny the power of imagination and perception to gain new areas of illumination and understand value. Schools are not monolithic, and inquiries into their workings and behavior cannot pretend they are. Clifford Geertz (1973), in his *Interpretation of Cultures*, poses that "the instruments of reasoning are changing and society is less and less represented as an elaborate machine or a quasi-organism than as a serious game, [or] a sidewalk drama" (p. 27). For a long time research has been directed at analyzing schools as if they were elaborate machines that needed systematic repair or adjustment and little else. But schools and the people who inhabit them are not machines; they are, in fact, more like sidewalk (or classroom) dramas. And it is that realization that makes the use of qualitative inquiry significant.

For this reason, I chose to shine my spotlight on two California middle schools and ask the following questions:

FIGURE 1.1 Selective Views

The Far Side © 1985 Farworks, Inc. Used by permission of Universal Press Syndicate.
All rights reserved.

- What are teachers' goals and beliefs about professional communities?
- What experiences shape these beliefs?
- What organizational conditions and processes contribute to the development and sustenance of teacher professional communities?
- What are teacher professional communities like and how are they perceived by reformers, by teachers, and by administrators?

In order to explore these questions, I conducted case studies of groups of teachers in two California middle schools in which teachers and administrators were explicit about their commitments to fostering teacher professional communities. This section provides an overview of the research method for the purpose of understanding the nature of the study and its findings, described in the coming chapters (for further details pertaining to the data collection and analysis, see the Appendix). All descriptions and vignettes in subsequent chapters were captured from field notes and audiotapes. The quotations are verbatim. Names of schools, teachers, administrators, and all geographical references are pseudonyms. Whereas earlier research has focused on school structures best suited for the formation of teacher professional communities (Johnson, 1990; Little, 1984; Rosenholtz, 1989), this study assumed that teacher professional communities must be considered in the context of teachers' collective experiences, beliefs, and understandings as well as their working conditions.

Why Case Studies?

Case studies allow for the gathering of in-depth descriptions of working groups of teachers and their relationship to the school and to each other. Qualitative case studies can be ethnographic, historical, psychological, or sociological (Merriam, 1988). This research, though not a strict ethnography, used ethnographic techniques (Wolcott, 1985, 1994), including participant observation and interviewing. Ethnographic case studies differ from the other disciplinary categories primarily through a concern for "cultural context" (Merriam, 1988). Understanding this context is essential in understanding the nature of teacher professional communities.

Why Middle Schools?

Middle schools are ideal settings for studying teacher professional communities. Typically comprised of sixth, seventh, and eighth grades, middle schools seek to better serve youngsters in transition from childhood to adolescence by creating a more nurturing environment. Through the use of teams of teachers and students, flexible scheduling, and collaboration between administration and faculty, middle schools emphasize familiarity, personalization, and social development among students. They maintain a commitment to intimacy long associated with elementary schools while incorporating much of the organizational features of high schools. In short, they are hybrids of the two organizational schemas.

As Paul George (1983) in a report for the National Middle School Association writes, middle-school teachers find themselves involved in a professional community of shared concerns, rather than being isolated in self-contained classrooms or assigned to departments where their common concerns may be limited to the scope and sequence of a single subject area . . . the entire school experience for teachers becomes more unified and connected. (p. 77)

In addition, studies indicate that teachers working in middle schools share stronger collegial relationships, have higher job satisfaction, and are more committed to teaching than those in traditionally organized junior high schools (Ashton, Doda, Webb, Olejnik, & McAuliffe, 1981; Bryan & Erickson, 1970; McGee & Blackburn, 1979; Pook, 1981).

Studying two California middle schools offers an additional benefit. In 1985, the office of the California Superintendent of Public Instruction commissioned a report on the reform agenda for grades six, seven, and eight. *Caught in the Middle* was produced by the California Middle Grade Task Force (1987) and culminated a year of research and public hearings on the middle grades in California. Outlining 22 principles of middle-grade education, it has served as a reform agenda. This focus includes the following issues that, note the authors of the report, "should be addressed in structuring effective middle grade education" (p. 100):

- Large schools need to be divided into smaller, more easily managed units . . . to allow a sense of closeness to develop.
- Curriculum organization and course scheduling should facilitate schoolwide planning for teachers, irrespective of subject-area assignments.
- Teachers should be provided with common planning time when their instructional responsibilities require coordination.
- The school schedule must be the product of professional collaboration and reflect an expression of consensus.
- Teachers and principals should participate in comprehensive, well-planned, long-range staff development programs which emphasize professional collegiality.

(California State Dept. of Education,
Middle Grade Task Force, 1987, pp. 100–101)

Many of these recommendations, directed specifically toward California middle schools, derive from or are consistent with reform efforts to foster teacher professional communities across the nation. This makes California middle schools a particularly interesting location for examining teacher professional communities in practice. Both C. Wright Mills and Louis Brandeis, the two middle schools studied, have embraced part or all of the recommendations in *Caught in the Middle*.

Broader reform efforts in California schools have import as well. In the 1980s, California undertook what one newspaper called "the most dramatic transformation of the nation's schools in almost a century." A range of initiatives swept the state as experiments with site-based decision making, alternative assessment, and reorganizing the school day were hailed as models for other states. The success of these initiatives varied tremendously (Fine, 1986). By the end of the decade, the late Ernest Boyer, director of the Carnegie Foundation for the Advancement of Teaching, had remarked that "the current movement is more public, more sustained and more broad-based than any that has taken place in the history of this country. California is at the very cutting edge of giving structure and direction to the essential questions in education" (Boyer, 1990, p. 12).

One of the more recognizable efforts to restructure California schools came in the form of Senate Bill 1274 (SB 1274). In March of 1989, then chair of the Senate Education Committee, Gary Hart, introduced SB 1274, which provided funding for schools to voluntarily restructure themselves. The bill required minimally that the schools address four areas for improvement: instruction, curriculum, and assessment; redesigned school governance roles for teachers and parents; new options for students after tenth grade; and technological innovation. SB 1274 went into effect in January 1991. Both C. Wright Mills and Louis Brandeis are SB 1274 restructuring schools (though as we will see in the chapters that follow, the evidence of restructuring is far more dramatic at Mills than at Brandeis).

Criteria for Site Selection

Two concerns—an expressed commitment to teacher professional community and recognition by local educators as having strong teacher professional community—guided the choice of schools for this study. Informal discussions with principals, teachers, district administrators, and researchers provided a sense of various schools' commitment to teacher professional community. I also read reports, research profiles, newspaper articles, school and district bulletins, and newsletters to determine the school's emphasis on teacher community. After visiting a number of schools, I found two likely to manifest the features of teacher community that were consistent with my initial working definition.

Choosing both schools at the same level (middle schools) diminished variation across the sites due to different organization, subjects taught, age of students, and so forth. Since middle schools are committed to more personalized settings for both teachers and learners, maintaining the school level constant highlighted subtler differences within the particular schools that contribute to their respective teacher communities.

In addition, I chose two schools in the state of California to diminish variation across the sites due to dramatically different state policy climates. The schools are in different districts—one urban and the other suburban—to yield variation in immediate school context. This type of limited variation renders a richer understanding of the multiple conditions under which teacher professional community can exist and, in addition, characterizes the different types of teacher communities that exist in these two distinct settings.

Limitations

The case-study design carries with it certain limitations. To what extent can the findings be generalized beyond these particular cases? Do the understandings of the teacher communities at the sites studied provide insights that have external validity—that are true of other schools and individuals? To what extent can we assume that the knowledge gained about the parameters of community-building at one site can be applied to another?

As will become apparent in the chapters that follow, the subtle and complex interactions of each school environment and group of individuals greatly influenced the findings. This is at once the strength and weakness of a case-study approach. Unlike survey research, which might involve a large, random sample representative of all U.S. or California middle schools and statistical procedures that can produce highly generalizable findings, case studies promise no formal predictive algorithms. It is not possible, for example, to describe with certainty causal links about the construction of teacher professional community. Instead, case studies provide a highly contextualized understanding of complex interactions of environmental, organizational, and individual variables and processes at particular sites. These insights can, in turn, lead to a deeper understanding of community-building efforts at other sites.

How? These case studies may contribute to broad conceptualizations. In other words, when we look at other schools, this study can provide a road map to identify what features of teacher professional community to explore—to suggest which organizational and individual characteristics are likely to increase our understanding of a particular teacher community. In addition, the findings of this study can be compared with other case studies to produce new theories and new understandings.

The findings from this study are not likely to provide the reader with a recipe for community-building at other school sites. No serious exploration of a topic as elusive as community could honestly make claims to do so. In this regard, I agree with Elliot Eisner (1998) that it is better to "appreciate the complexity of a complex problem than to be seduced by simplistic remedies that cannot work" (p. 60). In the next two chapters, I describe two very different teacher communities. Both engender some or all of the five features of community that I described in this chapter, though each one in varying ways and degrees. What these descriptions and analyses accomplish is to provide the reader with a greater understanding of the dilemmas, quandaries, and mysteries that those working to build professional communities in schools face and, in so doing, clarify for researchers, policymakers, and practitioners interested in building teacher communities the benefits and obstacles likely to be encountered.

CONCLUSION

Based on the conceptual and reform literature detailed in this chapter, I argue that efforts to promote teacher communities in schools are driven by a variety of underconceptualized visions of the ideal school workplace. Policy recommendations for improving schools often suffer from a lack of clarity over which professional norms teachers should pursue. Should reformers establish national professional boards to certify teachers? Encourage in-school peer evaluations? Restructure the school day? In each policy question, the measure of success depends heavily on the notion of professional community that teachers and reformers uncritically embrace.

I am persuaded, as are many reformers, by the rhetoric of community as a basis for school reform. Earlier studies, however, demonstrate the persistence of professional norms that run counter to the rhetoric and creation of such communities. Detailed descriptions of teacher professional communities in practice can help researchers and practitioners alike reconsider the understandings of and approaches to school reform efforts. The chapters that follow shed light on the possibilities and pitfalls of current policies for building teacher professional communities in schools. After a detailed exploration of community-building efforts in two schools, I provide a model for differentiating teacher communities in practice.

Until the goals, conditions, and processes for community-building are made more explicit and more is learned about how to nurture such communities, organizational reforms designed to facilitate stronger teacher communities may be misguided, producing further disappointment over improving schools. If schools are to pursue such communities successfully, then researchers and policymakers should profit from learning how teachers view their workplace, how they define community, and how they struggle with the dilemmas of building professional communities amid competing visions.

CHAPTER 2

Louis Brandeis
Middle School

BY 7:15 A.M. the traffic on Bayland County's largest thoroughfare is bumper-to-bumper. The early morning congestion offers a sharp contrast to the nearly vacant 7:20 bus departing from the train station, half a mile away. In line at the Healthy Foods Market downtown, on the east side of the thoroughfare, a father, dressed in a suit and carrying a briefcase, gives his daughter money to buy lunch and asks her what time she needs to meet the 84 bus. The 13-year-old's "I can take care of my *own* schedule Dad," is followed only by a calm "I know you can."

Jim Ordes does not have to battle the traffic, nor does he need to match his schedule to the sparse array of morning bus departures. He lives nearby, on a quiet, tree-lined street, a few blocks from Brandeis Middle School, one of Bayland's two middle schools, where he has been teaching sixth grade for the past three years. Jim arrives at school in time for a 7:30 A.M. meeting of the Leadership Team, a committee that makes budget, curricular, and policy decisions for the school. On the way to the meeting, Jim walks into the classroom adjacent to his and finds Angela Thagard already preparing for the day's lessons.

"So your kids will come over to my room second period?" Jim checks as he picks up a model of a tomb that one of Angela's students made for a unit on Ancient Egypt.

"Jay is going to come too. Is that okay?" Angela asks about the student teacher working with her.

"The more the merrier," Jim replies as he returns the model to its display shelf and walks through the classroom and out the second door on the other side toward his meeting. Last spring, Jim was chosen by Brandeis' principal to be one of two instructional supervisors (IS) for the sixth grade, a position that, in accordance with the school's policies, includes him among members of the Leadership Team. When one of the ISs moved to a district position last year, three of the sixth-grade teachers applied to take her place, and the principal chose Jim. Angela is Jim's "team" partner. Together, they plan curriculum and discuss the progress of each other's students.

"Hi Jim." Valerie Sionne is walking with a handful of mail and a cup of coffee. She was the other IS for the sixth grade last year and continues in the position this year. "Is there anything in particular you want to bring up at the sixth-grade meeting?"

"Nope, you decide," Jim says. "I'll facilitate if you want," he adds as he walks briskly down the outdoor corridor.

"I'll see you at the [Leadership Team] meeting in a minute. I just want to put this stuff down." Valerie raises her hand full of mail.

Just as Valerie enters her classroom, Melissa—Valerie's team partner—comes in to join her. Melissa's sixth-grade classroom is adjoined to Valerie's via a small, two-doored sixth-grade office sandwiched in between.

Valerie's classroom is bright and airy with its northern wall made up mostly of large windows. The teacher's desk is off to one side of the room facing seven clusters of four desks each. Melissa sits down in the reading area, a section of the room furnished with a couch, several comfortable chairs, and a carpet. Beneath the wall of windows, formica and wood comprise a white counter that stretches from the front to the back wall. And interrupting the even expanse of the counter, on the side of the room, is a large white sink of the sort that one might expect to find in an arts-and-crafts classroom. As Melissa and Valerie talk briefly about a lesson Melissa is going to teach that day, Valerie gathers a notebook and the agenda for the Leadership Team meeting.

Brandeis' sixth grade is administratively distinct from the rest of the school. While the seventh- and eighth-grade faculties are split into subject matter departments (math, social studies, etc.), the sixth-grade faculty is treated as its own "department," almost as though it were a separate school-within-a-school. Unlike the seventh- and eighth-grade teachers, the 11 sixth-grade teachers share preparatory periods. All 11 are paired into teams (with four teams of 2 and one team of 3). This morning, like most, 9 of the 11 sixth-grade teachers are in before school starts—in the main office checking their mail and phoning parents, in their own classrooms planning or looking at student work, or in the classroom of one of their colleagues.

By 8:05 A.M. Brandeis is awash with the noises and colors of 930 sixth, seventh, and eighth graders catching up on worthwhile happenings.

Brandeis Middle School, part of the Bayland Unified School District, is situated on a 26-acre plot of land amidst tree-lined streets. Lake, a street with a moderate amount of traffic headed for the larger Bifield Avenue, flanks the school's north side, while Greenwich dead-ends into Brandeis' driveway on the west. Parents are repeatedly urged to let their children out only in the driveway and not on the potentially dangerous Lake, but, on any given morning, swerving traffic and skateboards remain a daily headache for school administrators; accidents, on occasion deadly ones, have been an unfortunate part of the school's history.

The school is made up of several long, classroom-wide buildings, a few of which are connected via "the breezeway," an indoor/outdoor hallway constructed mostly of glass. Between the buildings are walls lined with lockers, display cases, a few water fountains, and bathrooms. The classrooms are all very similar, with one wall composed entirely of large windows, and the opposing wall of plaster and cement, leaving room for bookcases, posters, and bulletin boards. The dull white and yellow rooms offer little solace from the traditional drab grey of the exterior.

Students' clothing provides a sharp contrast to the monotonous colors of the school. Punctuated in fluorescent blues, greens, pinks, yellows, and violets, the combination of North Face outdoor clothing and stylish jeans with zippered ankles far outshines sporadic attempts by adults to enliven the walls with pictures or colored paper. On any given day, a number of sweatshirts boasting the name of the nearby university are worn by young college aspirants.

The changing demographics of Bayland are reflected in an increasingly diverse student body. With a mean family income of more than $90,000, Bayland continues to be known for its relative affluence. However, 5.5% of the population now lives below the poverty line, and one in ten students is designated as limited-English speaking, representing some 17 different languages (U.S. Bureau of the Census, 1996). Brandeis' students—on average—continue to score in the top percentiles of most state and national standardized tests. In the last five years, Brandeis has twice been designated a California Distinguished School and been awarded the California Sustained Achievement Award.

On this mid-autumn morning, California's weather is characteristically splendid. The grassy campus is green virtually everywhere except for several large patches around the school buildings that have long since been surrendered to the trampling of students' feet. In the sunny, warm weather, the buildings seem almost unnecessary.

Jill Fullan, Brandeis' principal, greets students and teachers in the hallway. She carries a walkie-talkie and a clipboard. Jill was appointed to be principal for one year on a trial basis after the previous principal retired. Following the before-school morning chaos, the trademark of almost every school, Jill returns to her office in the administrative wing. Five minutes before the morning bell, Valerie, Jim, Angela, and Melissa are in their respective classrooms. Each is surrounded by students telling them stories, showing them homework, asking about the upcoming test, or posing the ever-unanswered, occasionally bold, personal questions with which middle-school teachers everywhere must contend.

Local principals, teachers, district administrators, and researchers with whom I spoke to locate schools for this study all agreed that Brandeis' sixth-grade faculty—who work in teams, attend weekly sixth-grade faculty meetings, and share common preparatory periods—are an exemplary professional community. Many of Brandeis' sixth-grade teachers have what so many teachers lack and so many school reformers hope to foster: colleagues committed to their profession and interested in sharing ideas (Barth, 1990; Lieberman, 1995; McLaughlin & Talbert, 1993). "We share a commitment to kids and to learning," Mike, a new teacher, reported. "We want kids to do well; we are all very professional. We want to do a good job" (ob89).[1] The teachers enjoy teaching at Brandeis, most put in long hours at the school, and they care about one another both professionally and personally. Judy, who taught in two other schools before coming to Brandeis, expresses the heartfelt commitment to teaching and to treating one another with professional respect that the sixth-grade faculty shares:

> I really feel like this is a blessed place to work, a bit of a utopia. You're treated much more like a professional. And that has all of

---

1. References to data collected are coded as follows: (obP) observation book data, page P; (sbP) supplementary observation book data, page P; (iI.P) interview with interviewee #I, page P. For more information, see the Appendix.

these residual effects on the way you teach and how you interact with your colleagues. . . . When you're treated like a professional, you act like a professional and then you treat other people like professionals. I feel a real mutual respect. (i08.1)

Through common preparatory periods, formal weekly meetings, daily informal meetings, and personal attention to individual teachers' well-being, the sixth-grade faculty at Brandeis maintains a caring, gracious, and respectful professional culture.

Teachers share a commitment to good teaching and to meeting middle-school children's need for both affective and cognitive development. "It's like there is an intense interest in curriculum and children and the essentials of teaching," one teacher told me, "and the teachers want to inspire kids to learn" (i05.1).

Such commitment was evident during the meetings I attended just prior to the beginning of the school year. Held at Valerie's house with a catered lunch supplied with school funds, these planning meetings revealed a committed and hard-working staff. Teachers rotated through a variety of activities—planning curriculum, discussing priorities, and debating the purposes of their classes and education in general.

In one activity for which the teachers had split into small discussion groups, conversations were recorded on large pieces of paper and then passed on to the next group. "I think it is really important that these kids feel supported from us. It should be a major emphasis in our curriculum," Rose said (ob31). Rose's view differed, however, from that of Leslie. "I like the idea of support, of course . . . but what a lot of these students need to know is math," Leslie argued.

"Some need to know math," Jim added, "but others need to get their parents off their backs."

"I agree," Angela added. "There's certainly no reason we can't do both of those things."

The teachers nodded and wrote "better support" and "strong education in subject" on the paper. After each group had had the opportunity to write on each paper, the groups reported the outline of their conversation. Several teachers expressed excitement at the goals they were setting for themselves.

Brandeis' sixth-grade faculty are also involved in district and state-wide committees and conferences on education and frequently attend them in groups, splitting up and reporting back to their colleagues. Several teachers socialize together on weekends or vacations. Most report professional satisfaction, a sense of collegiality, and a sense of relief that their colleagues are hard-working. "I'm glad to be here with these people. I don't know where I could find a better, more devoted group of people to work with" (i05.7).

In many ways, the Brandeis teacher community seems a model professional community, one in which the teachers are respected and respectful and students achieve high academic marks as determined by state and national standards. Indeed, the working conditions at Brandeis are notable. In contrast to so many faculties characterized by isolation, anonymity, and sometimes hostility, the sixth-grade teachers at Brandeis have achieved a peaceful and supportive workplace. Conflicts arise at times, but, most teachers agree, they "never get out of hand" (i11.82). To the contrary, at faculty meetings, in department meetings, and in other official decision-making settings, there is very little expressed conflict.

What are the origins of a professional community such as the one found within the sixth-grade faculty at Brandeis? How are decisions made? Who participates? Who does not? How are conflicts managed? Who does the managing? This chapter focuses on Brandeis' sixth-grade teacher community, the climate, its characteristics, and its limitations. I begin with the three-year history of the sixth grade. I then describe the sixth-grade faculty community by discussing each of the five features of community identified in Chapter 1.

BRANDEIS' HISTORY

When the headline in the Bayland newspaper read "Building Schools from Scratch: After Three Years of Planning, Bayland is About to Unveil Its Kinder, Gentler Middle School," Brandeis had already been an established seventh- and eighth-grade junior high school. The school board voted in 1987 to reopen another Bayland junior high school that had been shut down ten years earlier due to declining enrollment. District educators and parents used the opportunity to move the sixth graders from the elementary schools to the new middle schools in accordance with recommendations made in the California Middle Grade Task Force's report *Caught in the Middle* (1987).

In the fall of 1991, with the full support of then-principal Bruce Allen, Brandeis reopened as one of Bayland's two middle schools. Its broad purpose was to focus on the learning and growth experiences of early adolescents, those in sixth, seventh, and eighth grades. "Moving sixth graders and reopening the other school was a way to relieve the overpopulation at the elementary level," Bruce explained, "but it was also an opportunity to change the kind of program we had" (i13.10).

Bruce Allen was charged with hiring an all-new sixth-grade faculty and decided that they would operate separately from the rest of the school and work in pairs. While the seventh- and eighth-grade teachers would continue to be organized primarily around subject area departments, Bruce hoped the sixth-grade teachers would work in teams across disciplines. This decision had the effect of making the organizationally innovative sixth grade a partially contained one-grade school within the larger school. While the plan for the sixth-grade teaming was set in motion, few if any changes in organization or curriculum occurred in the seventh and eighth grades.

The principal's decision to create a different organizational structure for the sixth grade also had the effect of setting the sixth-grade teachers apart from the seventh- and eighth-grade teachers. Though the sixth-grade students attend elective afternoon classes with seventh- and eighth-grade students, sixth-grade teachers have far less contact with their colleagues in the upper grades. By their third year at Brandeis, the sixth-grade teachers were making special efforts to attend subject area department meetings and share practices and strategies, and almost all recognized their relative (and collective) isolation and thought it important to make connections with the rest of the faculty.

With the help of a hiring team, Bruce screened applicants and, following the superintendent's request, gave priority to teachers already in the Bayland district. The hiring process was not especially selective. Though more than 100 teachers in total applied, of those teachers who were already in the district, only 2 were turned down. Eleven teachers were hired, 9 from elementary schools within the district and 2 fresh out of teacher education programs in the Bayland area. Bruce explained his hiring criteria this way:

> My first consideration [in hiring] was how they liked kids. Second, I was looking for people who were flexible, and third, people who had indicated a real interest in going to middle school. (i13.25)

The principal's hiring guidelines were echoed by Valerie, now one of the two instructional supervisors, who was hired early on and then joined the hiring team.

The criteria, then, were based on broad personality characteristics and interests rather than on specific ideological or philosophical leanings. That only two Bayland district teachers were screened out through the process indicates that a majority of those who applied within the district met the hiring committee's selection criteria. The most significant criterion for selection turned out to be whether one was teaching in the Bayland district already.

During the spring preceding the sixth graders' first year at Brandeis, the selected teachers' respective elementary schools were provided with substitute teachers for a day so that Brandeis' new sixth-grade staff could meet. Bruce planned this in-service day (as they are commonly called in school argot) with the help of the school psychologist. They wanted teachers to feel welcome and respected, Bruce said. They put balloons on each chair, had badges waiting with each teacher's name printed, and "fed them all day long," recalled Bruce.

> We made them know how important they were to the school and
> how I respected what they were bringing to the middle school and
> the value of their experience. I wanted them to know that they
> would be supported as long as they were on track. (i13.14)

Several teachers recall that the superintendent came during the afternoon and talked about his vision of what he thought education at Brandeis could be (i03.6; i05.9; i11.6). Bruce and the superintendent also introduced the two teachers they had chosen for the two instructional supervisor positions.

During the planning day, promises about teacher decision making mixed with demonstrations of explicit hierarchy such as the choice of instructional supervisors. The principal's recollection that "they would be supported as long as they were on track" likewise shows an ambiguous commitment to teacher autonomy. The teachers were aware of the mixed message as well. Angela recalls that first meeting:

> I think that what happened when we all got together is that there
> was this sort of shining moment when we thought, "My God, we
> actually have some power. We have some statements to make that
> will be listened to if we hang together, if we have spokespersons
> who know what they're about and who are not intimidated by this
> new setting, who could work the system". . . . And it was nice, it
> may be the first time in a lot of our lives, outside of just parents that
> we work with, where we actually felt like we had a sense of power
> and that our ideas were worthy of being listened to by those who
> were in charge of making decisions. (i02.175)

The sense of rightful power and the idea that someone else was ultimately in charge coexisted as teachers went about the task of getting to know one another and beginning to refine the principal's organizational plan.

After an opening activity, designed to demonstrate the importance of cooperation, in which teachers needed to work together using puzzle pieces to solve a mystery, teachers took part in their first cooperative task: dividing into teams.

> People talked a little about subject areas they felt particularly strong in, in terms of skills. That was important in terms of setting up partners because if there were two people really strong in math, you didn't want to necessarily pair them together. Like Jim said he was not comfortable with math, and Angela wanted to try. So they teamed up. Most of us felt strongest in the areas of English and social studies and weakest in science. (i13.7)

By the end of the day, each teacher had written down names of other teachers and the instructional supervisor with whom they preferred to work. Many of the teachers who attended the in-service day remarked that there was little controversy during this process and there were "no hurt feelings" (i11.15).

Those teachers who were in town during the summer met two more times before the 1991–1992 school year began. During that first year, these elementary school teachers became accustomed to the different organization of middle schools. Most had never worked in teams before and were accustomed to having relative bureaucratic freedom with their students. Field trips, for example, were no longer simply a matter of clearance from the principal. Now forms had to be filled out and submitted with two weeks notice, and teachers had to clear the trip with other teachers who would be losing students from their classes that day. The most vivid memory for many teachers was of constant meetings:

> Bruce was asking us to do a lot. We were being asked to build all kinds of routines for things, how we did things, and attend meetings by the hundreds. For most of us, 7:30 A.M. meetings were new. That in itself was a major event. We were having additional sixth-grade meetings two to three times a week. We were being asked to participate on a variety of levels in the school that were immense. And whatever we did was being judged. Everything we did, whether it was wonderful or terrible, it was being judged. Because we were the new sixth grade. (i01.19)

In August, Brandeis teachers adopted by a unanimous staff vote 12 belief statements that had been drafted by the Leadership Team (see Figure 2.1). By the time of this study, there was little emphasis on the statements. I found the list in a folder in the main office of the school and in the annual report

FIGURE 2.1 Brandeis' Belief Statements

1. All children can learn, and are entitled to learn at their maximum level.

2. Students want to be successful at something.

3. Each child should have at least one adult at school who knows him/her well, with whom he/she has regular contact, and to whom he/she can turn for help.

4. The middle school is a unique institution—neither elementary nor secondary. It has its own special place in the education continuum, and while drawing from the best of other levels, must develop its own identity, purpose, and plan of operation.

5. Students do not learn subjects in isolation. They need to be helped to see the interconnectedness of knowledge. The middle school curriculum should be a tapestry of subject content, study skills, and personal development skills.

6. The middle school curriculum must be designed to fit the unique needs of young adolescents and have a balance of skill development with exploration and choice.

7. Middle school children need to learn in a variety of ways, including a range of teaching strategies.

8. A positive school climate contributes to and reinforces learning.

9. Assessment of learning should be continuous, positive, as authentic as possible, and presented to students in a way that has meaning for them and reinforces growth.

10. School policies should emphasize positive progress, reinforce learning, and provide for a safe and orderly environment, and orderly behavior.

11. Parents are an integral part of the education of their children; therefore, the school welcomes parent input and involvement.

12. People work best in an atmosphere where the decision-making process is clear and understood by all, and where, to the extent possible, people are involved in the decision-making process.

to the community. The statements were not discussed at faculty meetings I attended, nor were they included in the binder of information distributed to faculty at the beginning of the year.

Instead, the section of the binder distributed to the faculty titled "Expectations" begins with policy statements issued by the Bayland Board of Education: "The Board of Education has stated its belief that the behavior of students must reflect the standards of good citizenship." "Self discipline and taking responsibility for one's actions are among the ultimate goals of education." The three policy statements reprinted in the binder are as follows (abbreviated):

- Students shall obey constituted authority. . . .
- Citizenship in a democracy requires respect for the rights of others. . . .
- High personal standards of courtesy, decency, morality, clean language, honesty, and wholesome relationships with others shall be maintained.

In addition to the belief statements and the district policy statements, the School Site Council—comprised of the principal, the four subject area department heads, the two sixth-grade instructional supervisors, four parents, and four students—adopted the following set of school goals:

- To create a safe, caring, inclusive environment that enhances active learning and healthy self-esteem;
- To maintain a challenging learning environment for all students that fosters independence and encourages students to accept greater responsibility;
- To promote instruction that empowers all students to learn.

When I began my observations at Brandeis in June of 1993, Bruce Allen was in his last month as principal after more than two decades in the Bayland Unified School District. Jill Fullan stepped in as acting principal pending a formal search. During this transition, the 11 relatively new Brandeis teachers continued their work in creating a sixth-grade program that fit Allen's organizational blueprint and the school mission while taking into account their own interests and beliefs. The substance of these beliefs is the subject of the next section.

SHARED BELIEFS

"KEYS TO COOPERATION" begins the sign posted on the wall adjacent to Valerie's classroom door. Underneath are three classroom rules:

1. YOU HAVE THE RIGHT TO ASK SOMEONE FOR HELP.
2. YOU HAVE THE DUTY TO ASSIST WHEN SOMEONE ASKS YOU FOR HELP.
3. EVERYONE MUST HELP.

The teachers file past it when coming to weekly faculty meetings and other formal and informal gatherings in Valerie's classroom, the sixth grade's informal faculty center. Ten of the 11 sixth-grade teachers are seated in the reading area, discussing the sixth-grade curriculum.

"We need to pay a lot of attention to kids' self-esteem in sixth grade," Rose, who has been teaching for more than 30 years, says calmly. "It's a really important thing for them to learn. They have to know it's okay to make mistakes and to take chances and not be chastised. . . . They need to know they'll be supported in taking risks." Several teachers nod approval as Judy Denton, one of the three-member team of teachers, draws a parallel to the sixth-grade teachers' support of one another.

"The same goes for us," Judy points out. Articulate and poised, she almost always commands the full attention of her colleagues when she speaks. "We can't do it for the kids if we don't do it for ourselves." More teachers nod.

"Do you think we're doing that to some extent?" Jim asks, leaning his chair forward and into the circle.

"I don't think that we're doing it enough," Judy continues. "I think we should be able to have an expectation that we can communicate more with one another and just share where we each are. Not with a critique of how something should be done or that one thing's more important than another, but just supporting one another in what's important to each of us."

Rose agrees: "People are diverse and we're diverse. Let's find the umbrella, the common themes."

"I think we found out last year, when working on the assessment issue, that we all respect each other and like each other," Judy says. "But we do come from different places on any single issue," she continues. "We are all good teachers, and that's enough for me to know that we can take the risk to have a conversation about what we're doing in our classrooms."

"Just like the kids in our classes," Valerie says, "we are all different. We have different ways of doing things."

"But that doesn't mean we can't help each other out," Jim chimes in. "That's what I want from my colleagues."

Sixth-grade teachers at Brandeis share a belief in being good colleagues. Professional collaboration supports each individual teacher in his or her work and creates a collegial workplace. Professional relationships are based on shared commitments to teaching, to diligence and thoroughness in their work, and to children. Rather than maintaining a shared ideological or philosophical approach to teaching and learning—as some reformers have suggested is prerequisite to building a teacher professional community—Brandeis' sixth-grade teachers' professional interactions are based on broad curriculum issues, exchanging schoolwide information (the principal selection process, for example), aid and assistance (support of a new teacher by a more experienced mentor, for example), and sharing curricular ideas, strategies, and stories. I have divided the discussion of the beliefs that the Brandeis teachers share into two sections: (1) what beliefs are shared and (2) the significance of the shared beliefs.

What Beliefs Are Shared

Well into the 20th century, school boards patronized teachers, treating them more like children than professionals. It was common, for example, for boards to stipulate that a teacher could not get married, keep company with men, get home after dark, loiter in ice cream stores, or leave town without permission of the chairman (Tyack in Kirst, 1984, p. 151). Many decades have passed since teachers were overtly told how to act, where to eat, with whom they could associate, and at what time they had to be in bed. But the practice of patronizing teachers has not gone the way of the 10-cent ice-cream soda.

Deborah Meier (1985), founder and principal of Central Park East School in New York City, relates the following story:

> On my first day in a New York public school, I witnessed a principal scolding a class for crossing over a line painted down the middle of the corridor floor. The teacher stood silent. I quickly backed out of sight. The principal's tone conveyed something that I instinctively felt embarrassed to have witnessed. Not only were the children being put in their place, but their naughty adult teacher was being publicly reprimanded. (p. 304)

In many schools, teachers clock in and out for "attendance" purposes; often do not know in August where they will be working in September; have little choice as to school, grade, and sometimes subject matter to be taught; and are interrupted without warning by administrative personnel both in person and over the loudspeaker. Teachers frequently eat lunch during 25-minute periods, sometimes with children.

In the mid-1980s, calls for the professionalization of teaching galvanized an interest in affording teachers professional respect, and giving them greater responsibility over their workplace. Brandeis' sixth-grade teachers share a belief in the need for this type of autonomy in the profession and exemplify some of the progress made in this area. Professional community at Brandeis means a belief that teachers should have greater authority over the school, have greater autonomy in their classrooms, and have time to meet as a group to share experiences, discuss strategies, and make collective decisions that affect the school and their teaching. Teachers at Brandeis, in fact, subscribe to beliefs about professional community strikingly similar to the student rules posted in Valerie's classroom: They believe that they each have the right to ask someone for help, the professional duty to assist when asked for help, and the expectation that most everyone will help. They believe in allowing different philosophies and different commitments to coexist within broad, accepted norms.

"We're a real flexible group," a math and science teacher noted. "We all try to stay very focused on what we think the kids need, what's best for children" (i10.15).

Rather than focusing on a shared philosophy, Brandeis' sixth-grade teachers endeavor to respect each other's diligence and commitment. The appreciation for this kind of professionalism, which the teachers (and dozens of studies of teaching and schools) agree is all too rare, is indicated in statements like Jim's:

> It's great to work here. I don't think I've ever worked with as large a group of people who worked so hard and were so dedicated to doing the right thing. We might disagree about what the right thing is but everybody is searching and trying to do their best. (i01.1)

This respect for individual differences in approach to the "right thing" is echoed by Beth:

> You're not going to be punished because you didn't do what you were supposed to [what the group decided]. There's room to disagree and there's room to do it differently. So that's a comfortable feeling. (i09.16)

Even looking from the outside of the sixth-grade professional community, the school counselor observed that the sixth-grade faculty "each has their own style, and they're happy to say 'You do it that way, and I'll do it this way.' They have an easy-going attitude" (ob39).

In addition to a belief in autonomy in educational philosophy or choice of pedagogy, Brandeis teachers embrace opportunities to exchange stories about their practice. Sharing classroom successes and failures was pointed to by a majority of the faculty as the most rewarding aspect of working together with colleagues. As Valerie put it, "We all want to pull out the good stuff and share the failures and weep on each other's shoulders and boast about the kids' progress" (i06.5).

If education has a mission larger than the classroom for Brandeis teachers, it is less about pursuing a specific educational philosophy or agenda for social change than about spending meaningful time with children and helping them to learn. Accordingly, teachers' interactions emphasize helping each teacher to pursue good teaching and learning. The following reflection by Liz, the new teacher, illustrates that the professional commitment is to one another and to work per se, rather than necessarily to a coherent set of ideas or beliefs:

I thought it was very charming the way people sort of pitched in and helped for the Martin Luther King assembly. Valerie clearly needed help, and it was generally something that most people believe in, even if they're not going to stand up and say yes, "I fought for civil rights," or "I lived through it," or "I believe in it." They don't need to. It's not the way. But people just came in and started working. I particularly noticed the few people who don't say much about their beliefs about civil rights or equality or anything, just doing. Like Deborah, and Rose, you know just working, taking over and doing the work. (i11.7)

If professionalism at Brandeis is based on broad commitments to children and to teaching well, what is nonprofessionalism at Brandeis? Interestingly, even the belief in professionalism as hard work was challenged by the two youngest teachers in the sixth-grade faculty. Mike, in particular, was deeply committed to ensuring that he had an adequate, fulfilling life outside of school and that teaching not swallow him up completely. His belief in professionalism meant working professional hours, which he considered to be 7:30 A.M. to 5:00 P.M. It was fine with Mike that other teachers sometimes met until 8:00 P.M. since he was never "forced to do that . . . I want a balance, I want to have a social life, to get married some day" (ob89). Similarly, Melissa made a pact with herself when she started teaching at Brandeis to work no more than 45 hours per week to "protect her sanity and social self" (ob98). Both teachers stress what they view as an inherent struggle between their job and other aspects of their lives.

The response of most faculty to these community members was consistent. Some were jealous and felt that "they're going out and having a good time while we're planning and grading papers" (i09.23); a few resented the fact that the younger teachers thought the older ones were workaholics or that the younger teachers sometimes did not come to staff meetings when they had too much work; but, for the most part, teachers agreed with Angela's view that teachers need time to rejuvenate. "You can't pour from an empty pitcher" and "They need to have free time to do the things they like so that they can bring something extra to the classroom" were typical reactions. One teacher pointed out that the two younger teachers formed a bond based on their common desire to limit their work and keep it in proper perspective (i04.8).[2]

Leslie, on the other hand, was seen as having a more rigid teaching style that might work better elsewhere or not at all.

> Her style is completely different than anybody else's. And her style is also, in some ways, unacceptable. I mean teachers can have different styles but if you're hurting kids it's not a style that's acceptable. (i01.10)

This teacher went on, however, to note the ways that Leslie did contribute to the professional community. "So there are issues," the teacher acknowledged, "but I still think she's professional. I mean she's here and she puts tons of time in, tons of energy. But she's hard to work with and help" (i01.10).

Interviews with most of the Brandeis teachers revealed a degree of ambivalence about Leslie's "different style." Few teachers call Leslie a bad teacher directly, and yet virtually all mention her as someone who teaches in a way that is significantly different from the others. "She is more old-fashioned," one teacher said (i07.9). "Some parents do not like the way she talks to the kids," commented another (i05.6). Leslie, in fact, is well aware of her "old-fashioned" style:

> Students need structure and sometimes discipline. I give them that in my class because that's how I believe teaching should be done.
> . . . I am committed to the children, we all are, but we each do it differently. (i03.2)

In sum, Brandeis' sixth-grade teachers share the belief that to be a professional community of teachers means to be committed to children, to respect and support colleagues in their individual classroom endeavors, and to have some degree of control over decisions that affect teaching.

---

2. That without vigilance, teaching can rapidly consume one's entire waking hours is common knowledge to teachers (see Andy Hargreaves, 1990, for example) and in this sense, Mike and Melissa are quite typical in their concerns. Chapter 3, however, presents a portrait of a school in which the distinction between the personal and the professional lives of teachers is much fuzzier.

The Significance of the Shared Beliefs

Professional community at Brandeis is more about professional autonomy than about community in the sense of a collective mission and interdependent work. Just as a professional community of doctors or a professional community of lawyers maintains autonomy over practice and shares strategies and approaches at conferences and in formal and informal meetings, teachers at Brandeis come together to reflect on and plan individual classroom practice. In the section in this chapter titled "Participation," I describe a few relatively small collective projects in which the Brandeis sixth-grade teachers work together. For the most part, however, their shared beliefs reflect what political theorists call liberalism, specifically emphasizing individual rights (to pursue individual goals in the classroom) and responsibilities (to support colleagues in the pursuit of these goals).

Extracurricular activities by teachers also reflect dedication and commitment to students. Angela, for example, conducts a workshop on fashion after school while Valerie leads one on quilting. And professional participation outside of the school community reflects an emphasis on the belief that professional connections with other practitioners are important and beneficial to the faculty community at Brandeis. This is consistent with one of Dewey's (1916) measures of the health of a community: numerous and meaningful connections with other communities.

The belief in professional autonomy is also reflected in schoolwide staff development, which tends to focus on specific subject area concerns or on "personal growth." The former emphasizes the individual teacher in an individual classroom, and the latter consistently embodies an individualist orientation to personal growth privileging individual rights and responsibilities over growth through relations with others.

In a staff development day on sheltered English, for example, teachers were exposed to strategies for working with students whose first language is not English. There were some participatory activities during the workshop in which teachers interacted with one another, but the program was primarily "taught" by a consultant brought in to help individual teachers explore the issues around language barriers in their own classrooms (ob129).

A more extreme example of a generally liberal or individualist commitment to autonomy was a staff development workshop on stress management. An outside facilitator spoke forcefully and eloquently on the need for teachers to take care of themselves (not one another). "Each of us has to care for ourselves," the facilitator summarized halfway through the workshop. "We can't expect it from our husbands, and we can't expect it from our co-workers. . . . We need to hang in there with ourselves as our own closest ally." Since the workshop focus was on internal psychological and emotional causes of stress, community-based causes of stress such as issues of power, hierarchy, or the shared stresses of teaching were left unexamined. "We need to keep a strong boundary around our sense of self," she cautioned; "teachers tend to have dotted lines as a boundary where others can get in" (ob96).

The Brandeis faculty's belief in allowing for different educational and pedagogical goals leads to a particular form of inclusivity, namely "getting along." The criteria for selecting teachers were very broad (recall that only two teachers who applied from within the district were turned down). In fact, teachers elected to work at Brandeis before seeing any of the mission or belief statements of the school. Furthermore, the staff rarely disagrees at meetings, and even tensions that emerge outside of official venues tended not to destabilize the community.

Brandeis' teacher community is one with a professional commitment to mutual support and autonomy but without a shared commitment to collective work or a finely specified collective mission. While this type of professional community affords to all its members the opportunity to take part in a variety of interactions among individuals, it does not always reflect the ideals of community emphasized by social theorists. That a community should include the voices of all its members is one such ideal, which I elaborate on in the next section.

PARTICIPATION

Valerie, one of the two instructional supervisors (IS) for the sixth-grade teachers, is printing the agenda for the 1:30 P.M. sixth-grade faculty meeting on one of the two computers in her room and distributing copies. By 1:35, most teachers are chatting and waiting for the meeting to begin. Valerie passes out the agenda and informs everyone that Mike will be facilitator for today's meeting, a role that rotates each week among the 11 teachers.

"Who is going to be recorder?" Valerie asks for a volunteer to take notes of the meeting.

"I'll do it," Liz offers. She is new to Brandeis this year and the only nontenured sixth-grade teacher.

Valerie sits in a chair at the front of the U-shaped conglomeration of assorted chairs and couch. Mike begins with the first item on the November 2 agenda in which the group expresses public appreciation for individual efforts. Most Brandeis sixth-grade faculty meetings begin with one or more teachers officially thanking or recognizing another teacher for some contribution. Today, Valerie thanks everyone for help with the Martin Luther King assembly. She then congratulates Angela for getting a renewed New Teacher Mentor position. Jim mockingly thanks Angela for spilling water all over his classroom. The teachers laugh while Angela glares playfully at Jim. Leslie thanks Jim for "stopping by to remind me about the meeting and for chatting with me about things he had heard I was concerned about." Several teachers nod. Many teachers believe Leslie to be "difficult to work with" (i12.26) and sometimes disruptive at meetings (ob39), and both Jim and Valerie have made special efforts this year to accommodate her.

In five minutes, Valerie and Deborah together report on a university-run workshop they attended on student assessment for sixth, seventh, and eighth grade. "I also have a report here on portfolio assessment," Valerie announces. "You can sign up for a xerox copy if you want. That way they won't all end up in the trash." Teachers nod approval, and Mike moves on in the agenda to "Funds/Supplies."

"Each teacher can spend $200 this year," Valerie announces. "Jim and I decided to allocate $200, and we cleared it with Jill. You'll need to make a list for the district, because they will ask for one," she adds. Three teachers mention supplies that they hope to buy with the money.

"May I say something?" Leslie interjects. Then, in measured tones: "Are there certain restrictions on the money?"

"What do you mean by restrictions, Leslie?" Jim inquires patiently.

"I mean can we spend the money in whatever way we see fit?" Leslie responds inserting pauses between "we" and "see" and "fit."

"In any way that makes sense," Valerie jumps in.

"I guess it won't go far toward my new car," Beth jokes.

"Didn't I write this in the binder?" Valerie asks somewhat rhetorically. "I'm sure I wrote all of this in the binder. Does everyone check the binder at least once a week?" In Valerie's office, a notice binder is used to communicate information to the sixth-grade faculty. Teachers check off their names each week so that Valerie and Jim can know who read the week's news and information. Valerie often reminds everyone to read the notices. On most weeks, between 5 and 7 of the 11 teachers mark their names with a check.

The next agenda item has Jim's name printed next to it. "We need teacher volunteers for the principal selection committee. Let me or Valerie or any administrator know if you want to be on the committee. This is a good chance for site-based decision making, so we want it to be representative and inclusive."

"When you say inclusive," Leslie interrupts, "do you mean the process too?"

"Yes, absolutely."

"Does anyone feel UN-happy with the present situation?" Rose asks, referring to Jill Fullan, acting principal of Brandeis since September. Jill has applied to become the permanent principal.

"She is really out there in the hallways," Beth points out, "I really like that in a principal."

"Yeah, I think Jill is doing a great job," Jim says.

"I think Jill is on tenterhooks now," Rose points out with an air of political savvy. "We don't really know what her philosophy is."

Valerie echoes Rose's caution. "At the first Leadership Team meeting, Jill and Carlos [the assistant principal] really tried to get a sense of what we [teachers] wanted in terms of professional community and our work environment so they could be in tune with what we all wanted. That was very professionally respectful, but we really don't know that much about what *their* vision is. Jill is being very careful."

"The bell is going to ring in 20 seconds," a visiting student teacher points out as Liz, trying to survive her first year teaching, jumps to her feet and heads for the door carrying a stack of student papers.

"Anything else?"

Just before the group return to their respective classrooms, Melissa says that she would like people to share the specifics of what they do with very high and very low achieving students. "That's what I'm having trouble with right now. The enormous difference in where kids are. I'd like to know any tricks or strategies that people use. Maybe we could exchange ideas in a future meeting?"

"I think that's a great idea Melissa," Valerie says. Several teachers remain in Valerie's room chatting as students fill the outside corridor. "And don't forget to check the binder!" Valerie calls after those already out the door.

Brandeis' sixth-grade teachers come together for weekly faculty meetings and attend sixth-grade and schoolwide staff development days. They discuss school policies, individual classroom practices and strategies, and administrative decisions. In the faculty meeting described above, the teachers took care of several points of school business and shared information, decisions, and humor. The expressed purposes of meetings are consistent with the beliefs the sixth-grade faculty share. The purposes are threefold: (1) interact with colleagues, receive important information, and be recognized, (2) share classroom practices and strategies, and (3) make decisions.

Interaction and Recognition

Virtually every faculty meeting starts with an informal exchange of stories, successes, concerns, and tribulations. "It's nice to just be able to see people once in a while," Angela told me. "At a lot of schools, you just don't see any adults all week long" (i02.45). "I would say meetings and lunch are really nice times to be able to catch up on each other's lives," another teacher told me. "Of course, it's easier to do that at lunch than at meetings," she added. Most of the sixth-grade teachers appreciate the contact they have with colleagues, though informal interactions during common preparatory periods are preferred to participation in meetings (i03.3; i09.12; i08.4).

Sixth-grade faculty meetings also provide an opportunity to recognize individual teachers for work they are doing with their students or for some contribution to the school community. When teachers helped create materials needed for a Martin Luther King assembly, Valerie thanked everyone at the meeting. Similarly, when Angela helped Liz with classroom management, Liz acknowledged her contribution to the group.

While many teachers enjoy the opportunity to see their colleagues, others simply tolerate meetings as part of the necessary drudgery of teaching. Mike, the appointed meeting facilitator in the meeting described above, for example, recounted his thoughts about faculty meetings this way:

> I don't talk much at meetings. I like my classroom, and I want to get back to it. I like to hear the information and finish: okay that's done, let's move on. . . . When I facilitate the meetings, I try and get us through them quickly. (ob32)

Though not all the meeting facilitators (a rotating faculty role) describe meetings in the way Mike does, many make passing references to the idea of making meetings shorter, less discussion-oriented, and more efficient:

> There's always some reason to meet. I think a lot could be accomplished by just printing information and distributing it, but I

suppose things come up that Valerie and Jim need to tell us about. (i11.19)

Examples of shared information include the $200 stipend for teaching supplies that Valerie announced, the formation of the Principal Selection Committee, and the reminder about reading notes in the notice binder. Social gatherings and celebrations are also announced at meetings.

Sharing of information and strategies and connecting with other colleagues also takes place informally in hallway interactions and teachers' common preparatory period. The architectural arrangement of the sixth-grade classrooms, in fact, contributes to interaction and participation among the faculty. This was observed by one sixth-grade teacher whose classroom abuts another's:

> One of the reasons I think the seventh and eighth grade teachers don't talk to each other more is simply the layout of the school. They don't have a central place to meet and they don't bump into each other like we do. . . . Everyone, with the exception maybe of Leslie, sees each other in the hallways between classrooms every day. A lot can get done in those chance meetings. (i02.3)

In addition to connecting with colleagues and sharing information, faculty meetings and other faculty interactions are forums for the exchange of curricular ideas and teaching strategies.

Sharing Classroom Practices and Strategies

Though much interaction around curricular issues takes place during casual meetings between two teachers comprising a team (which I describe in the upcoming section "Interdependence"), the sixth-grade faculty come together in meetings to discuss their ideas for teaching, and their successes and failures in classroom practice. In the above vignette, for example, Melissa asks her colleagues for their strategies for managing disparities in student abilities. Several weeks later, two teachers shared with Melissa and the rest of the sixth-grade teachers their thoughts on the problem. One suggested a way of having the class work on projects that all seem similar in scope, but can actually target different areas of study depending on the needs of the particular students. She gave several examples. Another described something he had done in his classroom that allowed students to work at their own pace but still share discussion. Valerie and Deborah also shared their experience at the workshop on student assessment they attended.

Similarly, Jim described a brief presentation he made at a faculty meeting:

> I did this oceanography unit, and I showed everyone how to integrate materials and use the technology. People told me that they appreciated that and that they really enjoyed it, and some went back and started using it almost immediately. (i01.9)

On another occasion, Melissa handed out copies of Edward Abbey's *Cadillac Desert* that she was using in her class and explained the points for discussion that could be raised from the story. "It's nice to be able to talk about some teaching ideas," Judy explained, "and sometimes you can really walk away with something you can use the next day" (i08.14). "A lot of [the more experienced teachers] have already given me lots of materials and lots of time," Liz, the newest sixth-grade teacher, recounted. "We've exchanged ideas and we're all very open and not defensive about our practice" (i11.2).

Making Decisions

Recall Brandeis' 12th belief statement:

> People work best in an atmosphere where the decision-making process is clear and understood by all, and where, to the extent possible, people are involved in the decision-making process.

Studies of organizations demonstrate that participation is greater when the stakes in organizational decisions are higher and when members of organizations can affect decisions that affect their work (Bolman & Deal, 1988). The ways decisions are made (which is in itself a form of participation) and the ways teachers participate in other events and interactions, then, are interrelated. Furthermore, the state restructuring grant (SB 1274), of which Brandeis was a recipient, calls for greater site-based decision making and greater involvement of teachers. For the purposes of examining teacher communities, the ways individuals are allowed to participate (or are barred from participation) in decisions that affect the community are of great importance to the vitality of the community (Dewey, 1938; Selznick, 1992).

I have already described the ways teachers participate in sharing curricular ideas, supporting one another, and socializing. Making decisions, on the other hand, engenders a different type of participation and reveals several important organizational conditions and resulting practices. First, Brandeis' sixth-grade teachers are allowed to participate in certain decisions, but not in others; second, teachers are strongly encouraged to participate in those decisions for which they are responsible; third, though encouraged to participate, teachers often prefer to remain silent.

In the earlier section recounting the sixth-grade's history, I described the mix of encouragement for teacher participation with exercise of an explicit hierarchy that characterized the sixth grade's founding. The instructional supervisors, Valerie and Jim, for example, were not elected by the faculty. They were chosen by the principal. The Leadership Team of the school, in turn, is comprised of these and other appointed rather than elected positions. Similarly, in the vignette that opened this section, Valerie informed the teachers that she and Jim, with the principal's agreement, have allotted $200 to teachers for supplies. "You'll need to make a list for the district," she reminds teachers. These, then, are examples of limits on teacher decision making (election of leadership positions, and primary control over the budget). In other areas, however, teachers are given opportunities to participate in making decisions.

In sixth-grade faculty meetings, however, decision-making mechanisms are ambiguous. "I think it is unclear what the process is here," another teacher told me,

> For example, at my school last year they must have spent two staff meetings where people almost ripped each other apart trying to understand the difference between consensus and majority voting, and trying to make decisions. It was hilarious and we didn't have the time for it, but these were amazing discussions. And here, I get the sense that discussion hasn't really happened, and so it is not quite clear who is a leader and who should make the decision or if anyone really wants to make decisions. (i11.4)

One teacher noticed that "there have been no formal votes" (i03.8). Another said, "Sometimes I get the sense that decisions are made in default" (i07.4).

In the section on dissent, I describe the ways disagreements are managed in the Brandeis sixth-grade teacher community. What is worth mentioning here is that not all the teachers see a particular need for participation in many decisions. Many remain quiet in meetings that are allegedly for the purpose of making group decisions.

> [There are] noisy loud people who express their opinions . . . and the very quiet people who give over their decision-making power to other people, and the quiet people who come later and say things in private, but for whatever reason don't say things in the group. (i08.11)

Indeed, on several occasions for significant decisions, when Valerie or Jim or the facilitator asked if there were any comments or questions, the teachers remained silent. When the budget came up on the agenda, for example, there was virtually no discussion (ob12). Furthermore, nonparticipation in the meetings themselves (not attending them) is a form of nonparticipation in community decisions and discussion: "If I don't go to a meeting and something comes up, I would understand that my voice will not be heard, that's okay" (ob.90).

Voluntary nonparticipation is manifest schoolwide as well. The Principal Selection Committee, for example, solicited input from teachers. "If you're interested in listening to the thoughts, hopes and dreams of prospective new principals for Brandeis," an administrator announced at a sixth-grade faculty meeting, "please let us know" (ob129). Though the faculty was supposed to discuss the selection issue at length and though members of the selection committee sat in the library for two days so that anyone could talk to them about their hopes for a principal, few went (ob112). Rose explained it this way:

> There was an evaluation form that went around to everybody, evaluating each of the current administrators' performance individually. And then there was a selection committee who went around and asked all the departments to talk about and recommend whether those administrators who are temporary should become permanent. The process was not really a process. (i04.6)

Perhaps the most engaging decision among the sixth-grade faculty involved the division of labor. After deliberation on how to equalize each teacher's contributions to the community, the teachers came up with the following solution, described by Angela:

> Teachers were starting to feel overburdened with the amount of work they were doing or the amount of work that other people were not doing, so we devised a point system. Everybody would have to have about 3 points, brownie points I guess you could say. So, one person decided that he would take over the organization of the supplies. The leadership of a task force, that was worth a couple of points. Running a club is a point. And then there's all these committees that I mentioned that sometimes other people participated in too. (i02.3)

Participation in community affairs among the sixth-grade teachers at Brandeis takes place not only in formal meetings, but also in informal contact between two or more teachers during the week. In the next section, I discuss the ways these teachers rely on one another for professional support. Though the emphasis is on supporting individual classroom practice, several joint curriculum projects and informal "checking-in" take place during lunch and preparatory periods, which all 11 sixth-grade teachers are scheduled to have simultaneously.

INTERDEPENDENCE

"Sometime in the very immediate future, we have to talk about some of the kids in our rooms that aren't performing." Sixth and seventh period are preparatory periods for all 11 sixth-grade teachers, and on this Thursday, Deborah joins Rose, her team partner, in Rose's classroom to chat about some of the students they both teach.

"Yeah, like the kids that I was talking about yesterday," Rose replies. She puts the pile of papers she was grading down on her desk. "I had 10 yesterday who didn't turn in papers, and I had six today."

"You need to put those names down, so we can figure out what to do," Deborah recommends.

"I'm thinking of convening a C.S.T. [Child Study Team] for some of them."

Deborah nods. "The ones that I have turned in for CST are Darryl Rutner and Tricia Gonzales."

"I wanted to tell you that—what is his name, the little student I spoke to you about?—turned in his assignment, although it was half done. That's still an improvement," Rose says tentatively.

"Andy Spears?"

"Yeah, at least he did some of it," she continues, this time with more confidence. "Also, we should decide what we're going to do for parents' back-to-school night."

"Okay, are you free today and tomorrow, seventh [period]?"

"Yep. Why don't you come by here?"

For first and second periods, most Brandeis sixth-grade teachers are with their primary class of students. Then, for third and fourth periods, many of the team partners switch classes. Angela teaches math to Jim's students while Jim teaches computers to Angela's; Judy teaches social studies to Beth's students, and Beth teaches science to Judy's. This kind of interchange in teaching allows teachers to come together

with specific knowledge about each other's students, as in the conversation above. Not only are students presumably better served by a faculty
who discuss their progress, but teachers form relationships through their
shared responsibilities for students' progress across subject areas. Communities are built around these interdependent relationships (Blau &
Scott, 1962).

The Brandeis teachers become interdependent through their individual
classroom teaching of the same students. "Because I work in a team . . . ,"
Liz observed,

> and because I have two prep[aratory] periods during the day which
> allow me to meet with my team partner on a regular basis means
> that I am not teaching in an isolated way. He and I talk during prep
> periods everyday and informally lots of times. And that helps my
> teaching and my curriculum. I think it's very good for the children.
> They don't get away with anything without one of us knowing.
> (i11.1)

Team scheduling allows a degree of flexibility and calls for a mutual give-
and-take arrangement between partners. Judy described her team partner-
ship with Beth:

> We really respect what each other needs to do. . . . And so, for
> instance I came in this morning and she said, "I'm really behind
> with your class a bit." We looked at the schedule and third period
> [was shortened] by 20 minutes because of picture-taking, and she
> said, "Can we?" And I said, "Yeah, let's switch in the morning so
> you'll have more time with my class than yours." We do that, it's
> very nice to support each other in that way. (i08.11)

To allow team partners to consult on particular students and on curriculum, all of the sixth-grade teachers share the same preparatory periods (sixth and seventh periods) while the students join schoolwide electives. During this two-hour block of time, teachers plan by themselves or
with teammates or consult with other sixth-grade teachers. Melissa and
Angela, for example, are not team partners but nonetheless spent several
periods each week working on math curriculum together "because we're
trying to stay on track and support each other" (i02.2).

These joint responsibilities also contribute to interactions during the
school day. Angela enters Jim's class to announce math homework instruc-
tions (ob119). Valerie and Melissa exchange thoughts on Melissa's curricu-

lum (ob120). Beth consults Angela on a new unit that Angela had tried with her student teacher (ob293).

While curriculum units are generally confined to individual teachers, there are occasional forays into joint curriculum projects. Angela and Jim, for example, implemented "The Dig," a curriculum kit on civilizations and cultures. Each teacher's class "created" a culture of the past, designed archeological artifacts as clues to the culture's beliefs and practices, and buried them in the sandbox of a nearby elementary school. After "digging" for clues to both cultures, each class presented its findings to the other (ob74; nb78).

These joint projects are rare, however. Jim explained:

> Usually, we don't actually do activities together, but teachers meet to plan ideas for curriculum and then share that and do that with their classes. In other words, maybe teachers teaching science will meet and say, "Well I've been doing this and it's really successful. Would you like to do that?" Or plan certain units together.... Mostly it's just within a team. I can't think of any big activities we've done all together. (i01.3)

Most collaboration takes the form of helping each other with individual classroom curriculum and sharing ideas, strategies, and practices.

Despite the relative sense of connection teachers experience through sharing practices and strategies, and pairing with another teacher to teach each other's students, the sixth-grade teachers are aware of the absence of joint projects and activities. "Despite all of our collaboration," Melissa observed, "we are still isolated in our classrooms" (ob.10). The common preparatory periods allow time to meet, a marked difference from the professional lives of most middle and high school teachers. For former elementary school teachers (which most of the teachers had been prior to teaching at Brandeis) who generally spend the entire day with their own students only, the distinction is particularly dramatic. Nonetheless, the isolation that reformers seek to alleviate by fostering interdependence among teachers is diminished but not eradicated in the sixth grade at Brandeis.

DISSENT

The agenda item reads "Team Meetings."
"We would like teams to be able to have more time to meet during the month," Valerie explains. "So we were thinking of the

possibility of alternating the department meetings. We could meet once per month with our team, once with our house, and then with the department."[3]

Nobody says anything.

"Does that seem like a good idea to everyone?" Valerie asks.

Judy clarifies the effects of the plan. "So, we would only be meeting once every other week with all of us."

"Yes, since I think it's important that teams have some time to meet."

Another moment of silence.

"I think it's important that we meet every week." Angela voices her opinion clearly and quickly.

"Well, should we try it out and see what happens?"

"The period's almost over."

The bell rings and several teachers jump up. "Since we're out of time," Valerie closes, "we'll talk about the fifth–sixth grade transition [the next item on the agenda] at the next meeting."

Since the beliefs that Brandeis' sixth-grade teachers have in common tend to be broad and widely agreed on, public discourse does not often center on principles, ideologies, or purposes of education. Broad educational objectives allow teachers with varied goals and beliefs to coexist professionally with little need for communal agreement. One teacher's curriculum is rarely connected to another's, resulting in individual freedom within each classroom. Teachers teach what they want how they want, seeking occasional advice from but not coordination with other teachers. Professional autonomy in classroom practice diminishes the need for protracted dialogue on matters of great import to individual teachers. Measured by frequency of conflict event, then, Brandeis seems a peaceful, conciliatory place.

Differences in opinion, however, arise over issues of professional interactions, such as the frequency or structure of faculty meetings. I witnessed several occasions like the one described above in which decisions were made without attention to tacit or muted or even explicit expressions of dissent. Following this meeting, for example, in which the decision was made to reduce the number of meetings of the entire sixth-grade faculty to

---

3. "Department" here refers to the sixth-grade faculty. Administratively (across the whole school), the sixth grade is treated as one department with its own instructional supervisors and meeting times. The instructional supervisors divided the sixth grade into two groups or "houses" (one group of six teachers and the other seven). Pairs of teachers within each house (and in one case a trio) are called "teams."

twice monthly, not all teachers were persuaded of the benefits. Several did not embrace the sudden division of the teachers into houses. (Originally, the sixth grade was to be divided administratively into two houses, one led by Valerie and the other by Jim. Though the teams were divided by houses as well, the structure is rarely employed.) "I'm not really sure what it is that we're going to be talking about with 6 teachers as opposed to 11," said one teacher who did not say anything at the meeting (i08.9). Another, also silent at the meeting, later said, "I think a lot of people liked the idea of meeting less often with all of us, but we all meet in teams anyway, and I don't know what a house meeting would be useful for" (i10.5).

Another teacher noticed that "at the last meeting, and I won't name names, I got the sense that there was a decision made that one or more people weren't comfortable with. Maybe those people would have felt more comfortable with it if the process were clearer, whether it was going to be a majority vote or consensus or what" (i07.6).

One of the newer teachers observed that Angela had disagreed with the idea, but that no one picked up on her objection: "She kind of dropped out of that discussion. And maybe that's fine. You know, maybe she realized that no one was in agreement with her and she was comfortable with that" (i11.6). This teacher went on to generalize about the ways opinions are expressed at other meetings:

> I guess he has to speak for himself, but sometimes I think that [Mike] may feel something or want to express something but may not have the opportunity to do so. If it were a different kind of environment where he could write something or where he was specifically asked on a regular basis on what his input was, then maybe he could get his say. (i11.6)

The ways disagreements are managed now has a history among the sixth-grade teachers. Bruce, the former principal, recalls the way Valerie and her former co-instructional supervisor dealt with dissenting opinions:

> A lot of it was done privately, rather than through meetings. If the ISs would sense that there was a disagreement or somebody was really kind of out of sync—some people went through some real problems, transitions, concerns—they'd go off and talk with them privately. There were tears. There were heartfelt feelings, but because they were so skillful in helping, they made it through it. (i13.21)

Though Bruce witnessed many conflicts resolved one-on-one in this manner, several teachers noted that many conflicts might be better off discussed in a forum where decisions are being made. For example, one teacher, when talking about choosing which of the two appointed instructional supervisors she wanted to work with, wondered "Why can't I say to you that sure I agree with what you're saying. . . . Just be up front with it rather than saying it to everyone in hallways. . . . If there's conflict happening, get it on the table" (i03.6).

Virtually all the teachers noted that some were more outspoken than others:

> Some people are real loud and vociferous about doing one thing or not doing another thing. But then others who didn't say anything, just don't do it or if we decided not to do something, just sort of go ahead and do it anyway. I think we try for major issues to come to some kind of a consensus where we all agree to give a little. We don't do that a lot though, in fact, I don't ever remember a time where we just voted and followed that. People want everyone as much as possible to be able to do their own thing. Like [one teacher] would rather be quiet during the meeting, let people go on with it, and then she doesn't do [what we decide]. (i01.15)

Another teacher observed that "there are certain people in the group who are very vocal and express their views and others who will simply keep them until they're recognized." This teacher acknowledged that Valerie sometimes asked quiet people for their opinion. "But there's no systematic way," she explained. "There's no 'let's go around to each person to have them say something and have them pass if they want'" (i05.5).

On another occasion, teachers were reporting about parents' back-to-school night. Most were giving rave reviews of the event when one teacher said she thought it was awful. Afterward, she reflected on the meeting:

> Everybody says, "Oh, I think Back to School went really well. I hardly had enough time to cover all the things I wanted to cover." These are people who stood up there talking to parents for over an hour. All the parents' eyes were glazed over after 20 minutes and so were mine. So I knew this was a bunch of baloney. People came up after and giggled and said, "We appreciated your candor," and nobody really wanted to own up to the fact that the presentations were awful. (i02.3)

Contention in the professional community at Brandeis also centers around unexceptional divisions. The split between those teachers who devote endless hours and energy to pursuing an ideal vision of curriculum, organization, or assessment and those who want to protect their free time and their sanity by being competent, predictable, and thorough is one found in many schools. The latter group, though devoted teachers and interested in improving their practice, would prefer not to attend lengthy meetings or planning sessions and would rather not change too much about the curriculum. This split typically falls along the line between veteran and neophyte, old and young (see Lightfoot, 1983; Sizer, 1984). At Brandeis, however, the idealistic teachers are the older, more experienced ones while the young, new teachers are quite open about wanting to protect their time. The older teachers, most of whom were elementary school teachers prior to coming to Brandeis, are, in effect, excited about starting a new career, while the younger ones fear being consumed by a career that they have heard carries that risk.

MEANINGFUL RELATIONSHIPS

Relationships among the sixth-grade teachers at Brandeis transcend the narrow boundaries of professional colleagues. Teachers socialize together outside of school and care for one another inside of school. Several of the more experienced teachers have formed friendships while the new, younger teachers tend to draw stronger boundaries between their personal and professional lives, fearing that the latter may too easily crowd out the former.

Celebrations and Social Gatherings

As the bell rings signaling the beginning of eighth period and the end of the sixth-grade faculty meeting, Valerie suggests that the faculty all do something together for the upcoming holidays. "Think about if we want to have a party or something."

"I'd like to go to your house for Thanksgiving," Jim shouts as he heads for the door.

"Oh, good, we could use a turkey." The teachers laugh. "Think about it," Valerie repeats.

Whether teachers are getting together for Thanksgiving, the winter holidays, or lunch, plans for various celebrations are almost always under way. A nearby family restaurant is a favorite gathering spot for the sixth-grade teachers (ob59; nb119). When one teacher (who was also an instructional supervisor) was leaving to take a district position, the entire sixth-grade faculty went out for breakfast, told stories, read poems, and exchanged goodbye presents (ob12–15). Birthday celebrations often take the form of long lunches that run into the common preparatory periods (ob108; nb315). The conversation is almost always social. "Shop talk" tends to be reserved for formal and informal meetings. Conversation topics at everyday lunches at school range from housing prices to current events to individual weekend activities and, occasionally, students. For many teachers, interacting on two levels—personal and professional—is a conscious decision:

> I think the most important ingredient for a team of teachers working together is mutual respect—which leads to some trust. Sharing on a constant basis, in all levels of life, whether it's my telling you about my kid who's going to graduate soon, or whether it's talking about making sure the curriculum reading is going okay. I think it's really important that we interact as human beings as well as professional beings. (i06.8)

A few teachers socialize together on weekends or during vacations, attending movies or going away together (ob126). These celebrations, social gatherings, and professional collaborations result in an ethos of individual concern and sympathy for colleagues.

Individual Concern and Sympathy

"When you've been out sick," Mike noticed, "everyone asks how you're feeling today" (ob91). Teachers care for one another and support one another with both personal and professional difficulties. During the 3 years that the sixth-grade teachers have spent together, several teachers, sadly, faced a great deal of personal hardship. When Judy's father passed away, she felt supported by the entire sixth-grade staff (i08.9). When another teacher suffered from undue stress, Judy decided she would spend every lunch period walking with her off campus to relax and unwind (ob62). When two teachers were diagnosed with cancer and were undergoing treatment, others stepped in to help:

> It's of course very, very traumatic and wearing on those people. But it's also very wearing on all their teammates, because they want to help and so anybody who knows about it tries to put out extra. . . . One person does not suffer alone. This is not a rippleless place, the ripples are immense. (i06.5)[4]

---

4. Rose, one of the teachers diagnosed with cancer, passed away shortly after I completed this study. After having taught for more than thirty years, Rose was set to retire the following year.

Teachers at Brandeis express concern, talk, and listen to each other and at times go out of their way to ease difficulties. When one teacher was absent for an extended period of time and could not afford the loss of income, two teachers offered to cover some of her classes so that she could retain part of her salary.

Teachers are of course supportive for happy occasions as well. Achieving tenure, children who go on to college, and appointments in district positions and supervisory roles have all been a part of the sixth grade's three-year history, and each brought congratulations, recognition, and individual regard. Individual concern and sympathy are strongly evident within the community of teachers at Brandeis.

CONCLUSION

The five features of community identified by social theorists in Chapter 1 all describe Brandeis' teacher professional community to varying degrees. First, the sixth-grade faculty at Brandeis share certain broad *beliefs* about education and about the ideal teachers' workplace. The most salient shared belief is the right of all teachers to teach what they want in the way that they want and to offer and expect support from colleagues. Second, faculty *participation* in the sixth-grade professional community ranges from aboveground participation (at meetings) to underground participation (casual conversations) to nonparticipation (silence). Participation in designing and implementing the sixth-grade curriculum ranges from an almost exclusive focus on individual classroom practice to occasional collaboration. There is frequent exchange of ideas, advice, and reflection, and an effort is made to publicly acknowledge individual endeavors. Third, *interdependence* is reflected in this kind of curriculum "sharing" and occasional collaborative planning. Teachers depend on one another for ideas and for reflection. Fourth, when beliefs differ among the faculty resulting in the potential for *dissent*, teachers are often allowed and encouraged to pursue their own ideas through individual classroom practice or to adjust their ideas to broadly defined shared norms. Breaking from group decisions is rarely frowned on. Furthermore, even teaching practices with which most faculty are uncomfortable are generally tolerated and rarely discussed in any official forum. Finally, *meaningful relationships* take place outside of school and there is general concern for individual teachers' well-being; the personal and professional relationships, however, are more or less distinct.

Teachers at Brandeis are part of a professional community characterized by an ethic of individual professionalism within a caring, supportive, and largely harmonious community. There are, however, hidden fractures beneath the easy-going coexistence. While there is little disagreement during official meetings, significant tensions emerge in less-public arenas such as individual classrooms and hallways. Some teachers refrain from voicing their opinions in official decision-making venues, and others refrain from voicing their opinions at all. Furthermore, commitment to broad educational philosophies such as "All children can learn" suggests, in theory, a common sense of mission, but results, in practice, in an enormous variety of ideological and professional goals for teachers and in a hodgepodge of curricular and instructional practices for students.

Is this bad? Is this good? I explore the benefits and drawbacks of different notions of professional communities in Chapter 5. My purpose here is to provide an understanding of the ways teachers at Brandeis work so that the reader can better understand the connections and disconnections between the faculty community ethos at Brandeis and that espoused by community theorists as well as school reformers. Specifically, when broad theories of community are used to examine real communities in practice, it becomes difficult to ignore the inconsistencies and tensions that are often left unexamined in many current studies of community.

Improving teachers' work conditions is essential to improving schools and Brandeis has, by comparison with many other schools, prime work conditions: a hard-working faculty and, for the most part, a hard-working student body. However, associations and beliefs surrounding Brandeis' notion of teacher professionalism, as we will see in the chapters that follow, can conflict with community-oriented ideals of democracy, real participation, and cultural diversity (Burbules & Densmore, 1991).

C. Wright Mills Middle School

A UGUST 31, 1993. It is hot in this barrio district school's cafeteria. As teachers hurry across the schoolyard into the south wing of the roughly U-shaped group of buildings, most head for the drinks table where fruit juices, sparkling waters, and coffee are on hand. They gather in groups to report the summer's news, to discuss changes in school administration, and to glance over the printed agenda for the next two days. It is early morning on a Tuesday, the last day of August. Though classes do not officially begin for another week, for these teachers, this day marks the end of summer and the beginning of the 1993–1994 school year.

C. Wright Mills is an urban public middle school with a student population typical of California city schools: 38% are Spanish-surnamed, 20% are "other" white, 14% Chinese, 9% African American, and 6% Filipino. Nine years ago, as the result of a desegregation lawsuit, the school was closed and reopened with an almost entirely new staff. Ten years after ranking near the bottom of district middle schools on average standardized test scores, Mills now ranks near the top. It has won numerous awards and attracts students from all over the city who apply— though there are no special entrance requirements—for a place in the sixth grade. "How does a school go from the depths to the heights in just a few years?" reads one local newspaper headline. "How Teachers Brought School to Blue Ribbon Status" reads another. For the past four years, Mills has received applications far in excess of its 650-student capacity.

The cafeteria where these preschool meetings take place is a dull, noisy room punctuated by four bright student-painted murals. Teachers eat a local supermarket chain breakfast: croissants, doughnuts, bagels, cream cheese, and fruit juices. A big fruit salad rests in a hollowed-out watermelon. Coffee is brewing. Ten Mills "tenets" printed on large blue sheets of thick paper are taped to the wall, partially obscuring the murals. Two flip boards bound the area where the tenets are pinned up. On the right wall there are two clocks, one smaller than the other. The large one reads 9:20 all day. Next to the clocks is a deceptively small bell.

"That's right, I taught summer school at Eisenhower High School. Very rough, very rough," says Richard Morales, the new assistant principal, to a new teacher at Mills. As Pasqual, a seventh-grade science teacher passes by the two of them, Richard reaches out his hand to touch Pasqual's shoulder. "I was glad to see your name on the LATA list." LATA is the Latin American Teachers Association.

"What did you expect?" Pasqual replies, barely slowing his progress toward Lena, an eighth-grade language arts teacher who is conversing with Anne, another language arts teacher. Richard Morales nods affirmingly as Pasqual reaches his destination. "¿Ya lo terminaste, chica? ¿La Novela?" Did you finish your novel, Pasqual asks Lena.

"Cómo dijo mi mamá," Lena answers, "La peor batalla es la que no se hace." The worst battle is the one you don't wage.

"Aren't you two proud of me?" Pasqual asks Lena and Anne, "That I'm here? On time?" He turns outward from the triangle to introduce Hannah as she walks toward the trio, muffin and coffee in hand. Hannah will be a seventh-grade math teacher, Pasqual explains. "She's in 7-I, with moi." He is referring to the family system at Mills. Mills' faculty is organized around six "families" (two each for sixth, seventh, and eighth grade) of approximately 100 students and a team of four core teachers who meet at least twice each week to make scheduling decisions, discuss the progress of individual students, and design thematically integrated curriculum across their subject areas: language arts, mathematics, science, and social studies. Both Pasqual and Hannah will teach in 7-I, one of the two seventh-grade families.

At the far end of the cafeteria, many teachers are already sitting at tables, talking, gesturing enthusiastically, and laughing. About a dozen are still standing, talking in pairs or threes. Three teachers stare out the grated window onto the school's inner courtyard. Each of these three stands alone.

As teachers continue to catch up on each other's summer lives, Tom Conner, the new interim principal, comes into the room, moving breezily through the crowd, greeting everyone he knows, smiling and introducing himself to those who are unfamiliar. There is a distinct giddiness in the air. Amid the loud laughter and chatter, snippets of conversation reveal a charged air, a mix of expectation and trepidation at the prospects of a new administration, several new staff members, an entirely new sixth-grade class, and, most of all, a new school year.

"Who the hell are you?" Though I was prepared for the content, the tone of the question catches me off guard. Lloyd Fisher, tall, in black cowboy boots with a beeper and an enormous keychain clipped to his large-buckled belt, follows his first question with "Are you a new teacher?" I start to answer as Tom Conner, the principal, begins the meeting. Everyone sits down at one of the tables. Mr. Conner, middle-aged with sandy hair, has an infectious lilt to his voice that he says is from his Irish upbringing.

"Hello. I'm Tom Conner." There is a pause. "I'm the principal. (Laughter). I'm going to be here with you, for the duration."

"That's what the last principal said" yells Pasqual from across the room. (More laughter). The last principal, Mike Gutierrez, was with Mills for one year when, in the middle of the summer, he quit without explanation. Most teachers have already heard this news. Some are distinctly bothered by an action they see as abandonment (i02.22; i07.12).

Lena leans over and whispers to Donna Trent, the eighth-grade social studies teacher with whom Lena has taught in the same "family" for five years. "I had the strangest dream about Mike. Did I tell you?"

Donna shakes her head as she moves closer to Lena.

"I saw him in a huge parking lot. There were only three cars and I started yelling at him 'Where'd you disappear to? How could you? Why didn't you tell us where you were going' and stuff like that. The parking lot seemed eerily empty."

"Speaking of disappearing," Donna whispers, "where the hell is Jeremy?" Jeremy teaches eighth-grade math in family 8-II with Donna and Lena.

"I'm not surprised," Lena says out of the corner of her mouth while nodding toward Mr. Conner to demonstrate attentiveness. "We should just mark him down as absent and call his parents when this happens. It works with my students." They both stave off laughter and turn back to the proceedings.

"So, what happened to Mike?" continues Mr. Conner. "We don't know. We still don't know. Someday we'll find out."

Donna says in a whisper, "Did you check the parking lot?" as Lena smiles. Conner introduces the new vice principal, Richard Morales.

"Hello," Morales begins. "I've seen a lot of you, whether in the Union or in LATA meetings. I'm very excited about working here at Mills. I also want you to know that I'm out there and active." Mr. Morales is a heavyset man with a bright, rotund face and dark, straight hair, parted to one side. Prior to coming to Mills this year, Mr. Morales explains, he worked for ten years at another district high school. This past summer he was the assistant principal for a summer school. "If it ain't broke, don't fix it," he says. "That's my motto. I am a facilitator. I help you out, cut through red tape for you, get you what you need." He finishes with: "I want to earn your respect."

Other teachers introduce themselves by saying something about their summer. "I sold my 1982 Datsun station wagon with 188,000 miles on it," says one teacher who spent several weeks kayaking and rafting this summer. Another says, "James and I got married this summer," an announcement that is followed immediately by explosive applause. Another says, "We just celebrated 13 years of marriage yesterday."

A few teachers talk about the tribulations of their summer. "It's been an intense summer for me," says the eighth-grade language arts teacher. She repeats: "It's been an intense summer for me. I did 'Connections.'" (Connections is a summer program.) "This was a summer from—are there any children here?—summer from hell." She tells about getting a flat tire that morning, picking her sister up from the airport, and several other mishaps and disasters. "So here I am, and I hope the rest of the year is not anything like this morning."

Donna Trent, an eighth-grade social studies teacher, begins by saying "I had a *nice* summer." Then, in a word that simultaneously defends her claim to a good summer and recognizes that those who spoke before her had less fortunate summers, she adds "Sorry." Donna has been teaching at Mills for five years. Before that she taught for two years in a private boarding school in New Hampshire, and one and a half years in Taiwan. Donna tells of a class she took on special education and her trip to Harvard with four other Mills teachers for a workshop on portfolios. "There were some problems and of course Mills had to make that known right away. . . . I also went to Maine and New Hampshire, and I went camping and saw rattlesnakes doing this dance, standing up high, wriggling. *I saw rattlesnakes doing it!*" (laughter)

Lisa went next: I "rested—read a little more, slept a little more, flossed more." Lisa, now in her late twenties, has been teaching eighth-grade science at Mills for five years. She teaches in family 8–II, with Donna, Lena, and Jeremy, who is still missing from this staff development day.

Pasqual taught during the summer, went to Spain and Amsterdam, and also participated in the Connections program. "My sister had her second child," Pasqual says proudly, "so I have a new nephew." He continues with, "This is the first meeting I've made it to. You see once I got tenure, I didn't come [on time] to meetings."

Mr. Conner interrupts: "It's a new ball game, Pasqual." (laughter) When Pasqual finishes, Mr. Conner introduces Sara Woo, giving her a rose for the work she did organizing orientation.

Sara, a sixth-grade math teacher, went to Nova Scotia for part of the summer. She also found it was "time for me to renew my driver's license. It's been ten years." She informs the room that they requested her Social Security number in order to renew her license. "This is the way the government sneaks in to get illegal immigrants," she explains.

Mr. Conner interjects, "It's not an immigration issue Sara. They just want you off the road." (laughter) Mr. Conner gives a rose to Elissa.

"At the risk of offending anyone," begins Elissa, "I want to thank Mark for perfecting our work and thank you to Donna, Sara, and others for helping to plan the orientation days." Sara and Elissa will together facilitate the next two days of faculty orientation activities. "I went to Italy this summer," Elissa adds as Lloyd holds up the photo album of her trip that is circulating among the staff. "You can all see pictures!" The album moves from Lloyd's table to the adjacent one where three teachers peruse the album together.

Lloyd stands up when he talks. A Vietnam veteran and long-time teacher, Lloyd speaks with a puzzling mixture of bravado and self-conscious caution. "After six layoffs, I am always insecure about not working," Lloyd says. He adds that he's glad to find himself back again this fall. "Oh, I was in Lake Tahoe," he adds, "where I got *quemado* [burned]. You know, the ozone layer."

Doris, the sixth-grade science teacher, reveals that she did not like her granddaughter calling her "grandmother." While most of the teachers are crammed around tables filled to capacity, Doris sits in a metal folding chair off to one side. As the introductions continue, Doris gazes out the small cafeteria window where a few boys who graduated from Mills the previous year take advantage of the last days of summer vacation to play basketball.

"I spent all summer trying not to be a grandmother," chimes in Raquel, a sixth-grade math teacher (laughter), "getting my daughter to take Pasqual's sex ed. class. I got reacquainted with my daughter," she concludes earnestly.

The introductions no longer require Mr. Conner to emcee. They have taken on their own momentum as Paul, the computer resource teacher, begins to speak from his wheelchair. "I quit coffee this summer," he begins. Several teachers congratulate him. Two jokingly question his ability to keep away from caffeine during the school year. "And I went to Thailand to help set up a production center where Thais can create their own wheelchairs that are light and low cost. There are about 10,000 Thais without wheelchairs who need them. . . . We can make this chair [points to his own wheelchair] for about $100. This one cost $2,200 here." Paul is interrupted by a jarringly loud bell signaling the no-longer-relevant change from one summer school period to the next.

After an introspective pause that extends beyond the bell's blare, Paul continues. "While I was in Thailand, my father passed away which was—" Tom Conner moves from his position at front and center of the room toward Paul's chair—"very difficult." Paul starts to cry. "My family thought I should continue my work in Thailand—[tears]—which I did." As Paul talks about his father, Conner first rests his hand on Paul's shoulder and eventually massages his shoulder lightly.

Eran is next. A sixth-grade social studies teacher, he teaches in the same family as Doris and Raquel. Eran, in his late 30s, wears a ponytail. Eran went to India on a Fulbright scholarship. "I learned a lot in India about Kansas." Maybe the only way to really understand your home turf is to visit someplace completely different, Eran explains.

"Did you see any cobras?" someone asks.

"You do get to see cobras," Eran answers. "But I didn't see them mating, unfortunately," he adds.

Donna smiles.

"And I just moved," Eran continues. "I'll be living in a house with 12 adults and 3 kids." Several teachers ask him about this communal living arrangement.

Another staff member says, "I was at the airport really late last night, because of the storm. I saw Pasqual there (laughter) and he drove me home." At 10:15, the bell again pierces the proceedings. "These have to go," exclaims Murphy. Many teachers nod approval.

It is now Walter Branson's turn to speak. The whole room's posture changes as this gaunt, soft-spoken, African-American music teacher stands up in the far back right corner of the room. Pasqual's *"louder"* draws a quick "He hasn't said anything yet," which is immediately followed by laughter. Walter softly, almost inaudibly, tells about his train ride across the United States. He talks about how much he likes trains ("almost as much as music") and encourages others to try such a trip. The pleasant adventure story is fractured with a rather grim account of the day during his rail trek when the train ran over someone on the tracks. As with the rest of his tale, this part is hard for many in the room to hear because of his soft voice.

Lena's voice comes in sharp contrast to Walter's. Lena, 36 years old, of Costa Rican descent, gets a rose for her help with summer planning for orientation. "I celebrated 13 years with my partner Judith," Lena says proudly. "Sign me up for 13 more."

Tom Conner again takes the floor to introduce Mark, who came to Mills seven years ago, immediately following the change in structure brought on by the consent decree. Mark has been teaching language arts and social studies for more than 20 years. "There's nothing I can do to repay this man," Conner announces as he hands Mark a large balloon. Conner shows the balloon to everyone. On one side it says "FEEL GRUMPY" and on the other "LET'S GET HAPPY." Mark spends enormously long days in school, during the year and on and off throughout the summer. He is often found at the school on weekends. His decidedly unglamorous and tireless commitment is known throughout the staff. What is less well known is that Mark is considering leaving Mills after this year. Like Walter, Mark also rode a train across the country. Mark travelled from San Francisco to Washington, D.C., to visit the Smithsonian. "No one got run over on this train," Mark says seriously.

When no one else volunteers to share a summer tidbit, Tom Conner again stands up front and addresses the staff. "On June 24th, I was talking with some people about what I would do next year. On June 25th I got married at Mission Dolores in that little lovely chapel there. On June 26th, Mike [the former principal] resigned. I am now the interim principal, and I hope to be a candidate for principal." Conner, who worked at Mills for several years as vice principal under two different principals, left last year to work at another school. He is glad to be back, he confesses.

"My first wife was killed by a drunk driver," Conner confides, "when our son was eight years old." The room gets very quiet. "My second wife—we were married for 29 years—died of cancer. ... What I take from those experiences is to enjoy every day as life goes on ... you can't dwell on the past. ... Victoria [his new wife] and I just moved. The whole staff will be invited to a St. Patrick's Day party. The wedding was small because it's my third wedding." He pauses. "I've heard a lot of things that went on last year. Whatever these problems were—differences of opinions, style—I am a good listener ... come in and talk about it."

"Will your door always be open, Tom?" Paul implies that Mike, the last principal, did not always welcome open discussion.

"What I've learned from tragedy in my life," Conner continues, "is to enjoy every day. I trust all of you to come talk to me when something is up, and I'll do my best to resolve it with your help. That's what we're all about here."

"We'll take a five-minute bathroom break," announces Sara. "Let's start again at 11:45."

During the break, two teachers go to Paul to talk about his father. Many small groups of between two and five chat in corners. Several cluster around the food table. Some leave the cafeteria. Elissa reads out loud from orientation planning notes to Sara, who writes furiously on the flip pad.

From the first day I spent at Mills, roaming the hallways, the classrooms, the lunchroom, and the offices; talking informally with teachers, students, and administrators; one message was clear: The faculty and staff are characterized, for the most part, by friendliness, a high degree of participation and engagement, and a love of place and colleagues.

The events described above and others described in the pages that follow are both ordinary and exceptional. They are ordinary in that each event is very much like dozens of others I witnessed. While I have chosen these particular scenes as clear and accessible examples, each demonstrates typical interactions among Mills teachers. They are exceptional, however, in their marked contrast to research that has consistently demonstrated the persistence of an ethic of privacy, autonomy, and lack of unity among faculty in many similarly organized schools (Feiman-Nemser & Floden, 1986; Hargreaves, 1994; Little, 1990).

Mark, a seventh-grade language arts teacher, echoes many staff members when he talks about the sense of common mission he experiences at Mills:

> I've worked in places before where there was a small number of us who always wanted to come to work, where there was a strong *esprit de corps,* but the rest of the school was often jealous and obstacles were always placed before us. Never have I felt that there was a full school movement together with a common goal until I came to Mills. (i12.3)

Through working on a variety of collective projects and sharing basic educational goals and values, the Mills faculty sustains a professional culture in which individual teachers' successes and failures, hopes and fears, and visions and constraints are all intertwined.

These qualities are both conspicuous and contagious. As a new teacher described it after one of the first faculty meetings, "You may be used to other schools and just taking a back seat and responding to others' ideas, or not saying anything, but when you enter this building, there's like a creative electricity in the air, and you feel mysteriously compelled to plug yourself in" (sb34).

Teachers at Mills are involved in an impressively high number of projects within the school. They typically sit on three or four committees, plan complex interdisciplinary curriculum, and attend (and actively participate in) faculty meetings, "family" meetings, department meetings, and community council meetings. Teachers often spend long hours at the school and several are regular weekend attendees. The number of opportunities for both professional and interpersonal interaction is quite striking. Most of the faculty report that they enjoy working at Mills and feel professionally supported, stimulated, and challenged (of 14 teachers interviewed, 10 report that Mills is "the best place they have ever taught" [sb96; sb22; sb57]; another 3 reported that it has its problems, but "I don't think there's any school that I would prefer" [sb3; sb18]).

There are also conspicuous tensions: perceptions of an "in" group and an "out" group, for example, and differences of opinion over decision-making processes or the degree to which parents should be involved in determining curricular content. As in most schools (and most organizations, associations, and communities), disagreements, disputes, and conflicts are talked about in the usual hallway conversations, emerge subtly and sometimes explosively in occasional altercations, and are manifest in gossip. While these typical "underground" forms of verbalizing conflict are present at Mills as they are at Brandeis, Mills teachers are more likely to negotiate conflicts openly in faculty meetings and other forums.

What shapes this professional community? How does it start? How is it maintained? How does it absorb newcomers? Along what lines do fissures form and who falls through the cracks? In this chapter, I discuss the details of Mills' teacher community as I observed it, its characteristics and features, how it came to be that way, and the different ways individual teachers and families of teachers experience it.

I begin with a history of the school to establish the context for the teacher community as it now stands. The discussion that follows the school's history is organized under the five features of community identified by social theorists that I discussed in Chapter 1. First, the faculty and staff at Mills share a specific set of *beliefs* beginning with ones they initially have in common and including those that grow out of shared experiences. Second, building on these beliefs, there is a high level of *participation* in a broad variety of collaborative activities, and individuals are recognized for their contributions to the community. Third, *interdependence* grows out of participation in highly structured joint educational enterprises that I will call collective projects and in collective responsibility for students and for each other. Fourth, *dissension* within the faculty and staff community results, for some, in the directing of particular talents and eccentricities toward communal goals and for others in the estrangement or departure from the community. Finally, shared beliefs, participation and interaction, and interdependence in the affairs of the teacher and school community lead to *meaningful relationships* that extend the more narrow notion of collegiality or professional community into friendships.

The reader should note that these categories are by no means distinct. One can see that shared beliefs are employed when teachers work interdependently on collective projects, collective projects provide the means for meaningful relationships to form, individual voices are made explicit through participation and recognition, and so on. The categories simply provide a convenient analytical frame around which to organize the discussion for this and the previous chapter.

MILLS' HISTORY

The first year, creating this school was like being in labor and giving birth, because there was a lot of pain involved; also a sense of newness, like having a baby that we were gonna all take care of together. (Lena Chacon, teacher)

Though Mills' three-story stone building and its adjacent two-story wing and courtyard were first built in 1924, both the staff and the district agree that today's Mills Academic Middle School was born in 1984. That was the year that the school closed and then reopened with a largely new staff under a court-ordered desegregation plan. As a result of a lawsuit filed by the NAACP charging an overly segregated student body and poor student achievement, a dozen district schools, Mills among them, adopted a set of consent decree tenets and agreed that the school would carefully note student outcomes and adjust curriculum and practices to suit a variety of student learning styles. Mills was required to "reconstitute" (the entire staff resigned and a new principal rehired teachers); only 7 of 40 teachers reapplied and returned the following fall (i12.37; i10.5).[1]

This process was not an easy one. Creating a common sense of purpose for the new school required starting with a broad but substantive mission—sufficiently substantive to make some teachers look elsewhere for work. As Celia, a seventh-grade teacher, remembers,

> The year before we became a consent decree was very very hard. There was a lot of tension in the staff, because the word "firing," who was going to get fired or vacated, was running throughout the whole building. Hostility arose once people started asking each other if they were going to apply to remain at the school, and the school pretty much divided into two camps. . . . Once the other teachers found out that we were [applying], they stopped talking to us. It was awful. Many of those teachers [who chose not to apply] had taught at Mills for 25 to 30 years and felt that this was just another reform, that yeah, they'd done it before. (sb19)

In the process of defining a new direction and purpose for the school, however, a strong shared sense of mission was developed. Mills the building remained, but the school would not be the same. Since the new principal had broad discretion over hiring and sought out teachers who he thought could work together to turn the school around, Mills reopened as an entirely new school, with a new faculty, and a small but significant set of convictions that the staff shared.

---

1. The case, Civil No. C-78-1445, was filed June 30, 1978, by individual black parents and the NAACP against the school district, its board members, and its superintendent. The complaint sought the desegregation of the district public schools. In the summer of 1982, the court established a settlement team to recommend steps for addressing issues in dispute. The consent decree included agreements that, by 1983, no school would enroll more than 45% of a single racial/ethnic group and that special programs such as magnet or alternative schools would be established toward these ends (U.S. District Court documents, December 30, 1982).

While the dissolution of the old Mills was wrought with tension, the formation of the new one was characterized by excitement and expectation. Lena, one of the eighth-grade language arts teachers, recalls the first day that the staff was all together:

> We had a speaker, I don't remember who it was, but there was this incredible feeling that we were brought together for a mission and it was very inspirational because they stood up there and said to us that you have the bottom schools in the district and you have to turn them into the top schools in a year. And this is what your job is. That is such a vivid memory . . . because we said, "Okay, that's our mission and that's what we're going to do." (sb3)

In part because of the nature of the task and in part because of the way in which it was implemented by the first principal, the creation of the new Mills was a distinctly collective enterprise, one in which the ultimate goal was inextricable from the community of teachers who shared it.

New teachers and staff subscribed to ten consent decree tenets or belief statements (see Figure 3.1) giving them an initial basis for discussion of educational goals and values. Each school year the principal and staff review the history and content of the belief statements, modifying them, if necessary. The collective history is thereby preserved while allowing for changes that reflect the composition of each new faculty and staff.

FIGURE 3.1 Mills' Belief Statements

1. All individuals should learn to live and work in a world that is characterized by interdependence and cultural diversity.

2. All individuals are entitled to be treated with respect and dignity.

3. All individuals want to learn and be recognized for their achievement.

4. All individuals can learn.

5. All individuals learn in many ways and at varying rates.

6. Each individual learns best in a particular way.

7. All individuals are both potential learners and potential teachers.

8. If individuals do not learn, then those assigned to be their teachers should accept responsibility for this failure and should take appropriate remedial action.

9. Learning has both cognitive and affective dimensions.

10. Parents want their children to attain their fullest potential as learners and to succeed academically.

On the first day, the new principal put a blank piece of paper on the table and, in what was a memorable event for Lena and other teachers, said, "Okay, what do you guys want?" All members of the new staff were encouraged to state what was important to them. Lena remembers insisting that all children have equal access to the resources at the school and that tracking not be used to limit resources to certain populations in the school, a concern that became a central Mills conviction. Another teacher remembers talking about the needs of Chinese bilingual students, while a paraprofessional at the time recalls her request to minimize class size in as many creative ways as possible. During this process, Mark recalls, it became "immediately clear [to the staff] that everything was a piece of the puzzle. Everything was not a thing to itself. You put your bit in and you understood it was a piece of something bigger" (i12.11). Moreover, knowing that individuals' concerns were going to be taken seriously allowed a climate to form in which "everyone kind of looked out for everybody else's needs while feeling that you were being heard and the little piece that was important to you mattered" (i01.12).

That everyone's piece could be considered important and that these pieces fit together to make "something bigger" indicates a strong process of integration. Each teacher's concerns were listened to and, further, incorporated into the mission and design of the school. The process started, however, with a group of individuals who share certain common commitments, which I describe next.

SHARED BELIEFS

All of Mills' social studies teachers are meeting in Sabrina's seventh-grade social studies classroom. On the wall above the blackboard is a large blue card-stock placard.

Three Essential Questions

1. What is social responsibility?
2. What are human rights? When and how have they been violated?
3. What has been the role and form of social protest in history?

"Awareness Month Vocabulary" is written on the top right of the blackboard with the words *xenophobia, homophobia,* and *racism* underneath. The topic of the department meeting is a "thematic articulation" across grades, and the focus is on curriculum that relates to the schoolwide Awareness Month—a specially designated period during which all the teachers at Mills relate the curriculum in their respective subject areas to issues of prejudice and intolerance, both within the school and in the larger community in which the students live. The six teachers are clustered around several desks in the center of the room.

"For my oral history project," Donna begins the meeting, "students interview their family over two generations." She explains the time line of the project and the types of questions students ask and then summarizes the assignment's purposes. "The project addresses politics in addition to culture," she concludes.

"I think politics are a part of any family in the form of power relationships," Eran points out. "One of the things students do in our oral histories is interview their parents about whether they or someone else close to them has experienced any kind of prejudice or discrimination."

Others nod. "I call it 'From Me To You,'" Eran continues, "which flat out comes from where kids are at this age." Donna and Sabrina signal approval with "uh huh"s. "They come in with a very self-referential experience, and I hope that by the time they come out of the course, they see themselves more within a society, a larger society, as part of not only their family and friends, but larger groups of people, whether politically active groups or just part of a larger social structure that they participate in."

Donna smiles. "And we hope they'll choose the right social structures."

"We do our best on that front," Sabrina adds, pointing across the room to three student-designed projects about gang violence. The middle one on display reports: "Out of 64 homicides, 20 are gang related." Underneath, it asks "Are gangs worth a bullet to the head?"

"Well, there's work to be done in this world, isn't there?" Eran asks.

After a few nods and some laughter, the teachers move closer to the cluster of desks as Sabrina tears a piece of white butcher-block paper from a large pad and places it in the center of the group.

While there is near universal agreement among critics of community that shared beliefs are an essential component of any community, there are surprisingly few descriptions of practice that allow us to understand the methods of sharing beliefs or the significance of particular beliefs. There are even fewer that distinguish between shared beliefs that are oriented toward communal attachments and those that are not. Conversations like the one above reveal that Mills' teachers build on a common understanding of shared values to create a collective sense of purpose in their work. Mills teachers' shared beliefs about educational principles, strategies, and practices engender a commitment to communal attachments and to the importance of relationships in community.

Beliefs in the Purpose of Schooling

Turn-of-the-century educators such as William Kilpatrick (1918), George Counts (1932), and John Dewey (1900/1956, 1916) laid the groundwork for decades of reform that sought to center teaching and learning around activities that were both authentic and consequential for teachers and students. They sought curriculum in which students learned to critically assess and respond collectively to matters of social consequence and hoped that students' values and beliefs might be transformed by these experiences. As Lawrence Cremin (1988) explains, these educators believed that "by manipulating the school curriculum they could ultimately change the world" (p. 187). Thus, George Counts titled his widely read book *Dare the School Build a New Social Order* (1932).

Like Kilpatrick, Counts, and Dewey, many Mills teachers are motivated by the promise of social and political transformation that schooling holds. They believe in teaching social responsibility and democratic participation. And they champion interdisciplinary, project-based learning, believing it to be more authentic, more motivating, and more effective.

"I think education is the vehicle that is going to allow this country to continue to exist," a seventh-grade teacher told me. "If we're going to overcome the Rodney King stuff and the [Reginald] Denny issues, and the handgun issues and the gangs and the violence, we had better start to think about having students better understand their world" (i09.29).

A simple stroll around the school confirms the social-justice orientation of these beliefs. On the walls between the third-floor classrooms of the eight teachers that comprise the two eighth-grade families, student-designed posters are on display from last year's Learning Challenges (interdisciplinary curriculum projects described in detail later in this chapter). The posters were part of a presentation during the Challenge Fair, culminating the special one- to two-week Learning Challenges curriculum. "People are like the colors in a painter's palette . . . you need them all to paint a perfect picture," reads one. "Free your mind," reads another, with

words like *sexism, racism, discrimination,* and *homophobia* floating out from
a drawing of a head into a garbage can. An immigration time line beginning in the 1400s with Columbus' arrival and ending in the year 2000 with
Central and South American refugees asks: "If we are all immigrants, does
it matter when we immigrated?" One of the decisions made during the early
stages of restructuring, in fact, was that social studies would drive much
of the interdisciplinary curriculum.

Teachers' shared understandings of the purpose of education are reflected in virtually every facet of the curriculum. From Awareness Month
to special assemblies to everyday classroom curriculum, having students
think critically about the ways they can understand and participate in a
democratic dialogue is of great importance to Mills teachers. Discussing
last year's planning for Awareness Month, one teacher described a preliminary activity designed to introduce to students the terms they would be
hearing in each of their classes during the transdisciplinary curriculum:

> We did a little take-off on Jeopardy and we wrote the script to talk
> about the Awareness Month terms. The categories were things like
> "I'll take racism for 100" and then [the answer] was something like
> "She was known for refusing to give up her seat and starting the
> Alabama bus boycott." (i01.52)

That these values are shared and made explicit allows teachers to easily plan together complex interdisciplinary curriculum that requires a
shared sense of purpose and to articulate that purpose clearly. In a booklet written as part of a portfolio describing their "learning challenges"
curriculum, for example, one family of teachers wrote the following: "The
most reliable way to prepare all of our students to lead personally fulfilling and socially responsible lives is to help them understand the present,
their present . . . [to] become informed and participating members in a
democratic, multicultural society." Many Mills teachers are drawn together
by their common commitment to some central beliefs about the world and
about the purpose of education.

This focus also serves to alienate other teachers. Jeremy, one of the
eighth-grade math teachers, for example, does not share the same political commitments as his colleagues (i04.2; i03.9). This is at times alienating
for him and frustrating for the other teachers. (The way they negotiate these
differences is explored in the section "Dissent.")

Convictions about the purpose of education such as inculcating a sense
of tolerance also lead to norms of openness among teachers around issues
that, in other schools, often lead to divisions and suspicions. Lena, who
began teaching eighth-grade language arts at Mills in 1984, the first restruc-

turing year, compares her experience at Mills with the school in which she taught previously.

> When I was at Parkside [pseudonym], I was very closeted. I did not let anyone know, and I kept to my own world there. It didn't feel safe to me. Even though I met two gay people that I worked with there who are still very dear friends of mine, they also knew that you don't talk about things. When I came to Mills, for no reason at all, the first year, we had like 17 people who were either gay or lesbian on staff. So this is what led us to start thinking about things like this Awareness Month you've been hearing about. (i01.15)

Many schools subscribe to clichés about the purpose of education. While truisms such as "All children can learn" or "Students want to be successful at something" might please a broad constituency of parents, teachers, and administrators, they are not likely to serve as a unifying or mobilizing call for the school faculty. Like the Brandeis faculty, teachers at Mills embrace some broad goals. Mills teachers, however, also share strong, specific, and pointed beliefs that enable these broader goals to have direction and purpose. Mills' mission—unlike that of Brandeis—is not to welcome all beliefs and strategies for teaching. Many teachers would not be comfortable with the Mills faculty's beliefs about schooling's purpose. Similarly, not all would be comfortable with the ways Mills teachers teach together or with the strategies Mills teachers use to move toward their goals.

Beliefs in Teaching Strategies

Teachers at Mills share pedagogical as well as philosophical and political commitments. They believe not only in schooling as a means for social transformation but also in shared pedagogical strategies as a vehicle for these beliefs. "When important ideas are embedded in environmental and social issues, in problems of local and global concern, or in creative products and performances," the booklet quoted above continues, "they extend the boundaries of any discipline." Pedagogically, lessons learned when grappling with real-world concerns and issues, Mills teachers tend to agree, will be more engaging, more authentic, and more effective.

Similarly, the teachers maintain that when learning is built around themes rather than arbitrarily divided by subject areas, it becomes more relevant and more compelling for students and teachers alike. Accordingly, Mills teachers expend a great deal of time and effort developing interdisciplinary curriculum within each family of teachers, providing further opportunities for building on old and developing new, shared ideals.

These strategies, however, are not only means to an end. The process itself reflects the principles of participation and social justice toward which Mills teachers strive. The beliefs Mills teachers share about teaching strategies—like those about the purposes of schooling—engender a community orientation to the educational, political, and social aspects of their and their students' work both in schools and in society. These approaches to teaching reflect the strategic importance for the community of broad participation and, more specifically, of bringing all the community's members' voices to the table.

A sixth-grade teacher, for example, expresses educational goals consistent with a community-minded ideological commitment.

> There's a very strong commitment to providing a good quality education for kids who don't generally have access to good education, kids who come from either economically disadvantaged or otherwise disadvantaged backgrounds and are at risk of checking out entirely. Most of us think that the country can't ignore these kids, that we need them. That is a really powerful underlying commitment in this school. You find little if any evidence that there are people who don't believe in it. And the people who do believe in it, believe in it so passionately, [they] have enough energy to cover three or four people [who don't]. (i05.12)

Another teacher talks about the value these students offer to the school community.

> We really try to make sure that all kids here can shine in something, that they can take part in the life of the school. . . . Sometimes that means that we have to look into allegations of homophobia or discrimination by students or teachers in order to make someone feel a part. (i07.15)

Both teachers highlight the importance of ensuring the continued participation of students who might otherwise be marginalized in affairs of the school and of the larger (national) community. At Mills, the content, then, and not just the form of shared beliefs matters when maintaining a community ethos. The quest for diversity and inclusivity calls for a strategy for ensuring that students participate.

Beliefs in Strategies for Working Together

These goals also call for strategies for teacher participation. The process of planning interdisciplinary curriculum for students (described in the

"Interdependence" section), for example, also encourages participation by the faculty. A vast majority of teachers not only are offered the opportunity to voice their opinions, share their talents, and contribute to the community, but actually do. Shared beliefs in strategies for working together such as teaming help to achieve this kind of participation. "I think I was really strongly committed to the idea of working as a team," one teacher told me (i09.8). Another described the ways he wanted to work with his colleagues:

> What I wanted when I came here was to work with people who were open to talking with each other about all aspects of a kid's learning and who would seek out each other's strengths and weaknesses and find a balance. So that all people were sharing the work equally and playing to their strengths and developing themselves in their weaknesses. It's the same kind of view I have of what kids should be doing in the classroom. . . . My ideal was to find people who were really going to be into [authentic and interdisciplinary learning] and who were going to be willing to utterly challenge the traditional structures. (i13.4)

Eran, the sixth-grade social studies teacher, described his ideal vision for teaching this way:

> I loved the idea of waking up in the middle of the night with an idea and being able to get real excited and call up somebody else and go, "What do you think of this?" and not have them be really angry that you called them at three o'clock in the morning. (i05.10)

Strategies for teachers working with one another also include sharing experiences teachers have outside of the Mills teacher community. Teachers' activities outside of the school merge with their activities inside the school, connecting the local Mills faculty community to broader communities at the same time that voices of members are heard and identities within the community are formed. Three Mills teachers have served as president of the citywide Latin American Teachers Association (LATA) and have made Hispanic concerns a part of their role in the school. Others are involved in political work around issues of gay and lesbian rights and have found the Mills faculty receptive. One year, World AIDS day fell during Awareness Month, and several Mills teachers involved in organizing for the event also organized a schoolwide assembly. Another group planned a culminating assembly for Awareness Month intended to raise the understanding of issues surrounding immigration and Proposition 187, a California ballot measure that many of the teachers consider overtly racist (ob66). Other groups have planned forums on Los Angeles and Rodney King and on the status of women (sb10). Frequently, at the end of faculty meetings, teachers or administrators announce community events that might interest other faculty and staff. During the California debates over Proposition 187, for example, Richard Morales, the assistant principal, announced a meeting of the Latino Coalition as well as a rally at City Hall (sb24).

How Shared Beliefs Are Identified and Used to Build Community

The beliefs that are shared among the Mills faculty—beliefs about (1) the purpose of school, (2) pedagogical strategies for working toward this purpose, and (3) strategies for teachers working together that emphasize participation—engender a community orientation. These beliefs, however, constitute only the "what do they strive for" of Mills' professional community. The remainder of this section, and much of the rest of this chapter, addresses the more difficult "how" question: How do Mills teachers move toward these shared beliefs and shared goals? Both the school design and curriculum development as well as careful hiring reflect concern for meaningful relationships, social and collegial interdependence, and community participation—what Benjamin Barber (1984) calls "strong democracy."

"What [people] must have in common in order to form a community," John Dewey wrote in 1916, "are aims, beliefs, aspirations, knowledge—a common understanding—like-mindedness as the sociologists say" (p. 4). In this quotation, he appears to be arguing for some degree of selectivity if a community is to be successful. Yet he goes on to assert that to develop these commonalities, we need communication that "secures similar emotional and intellectual dispositions" (p. 4). Which is it? Do communities need to be careful about the preexisting beliefs of their constituent members to ensure that they are "like-minded"? Or do communities need structures and processes in place that draw on commonalities and unify a potentially disparate membership? Evidence from the Mills teacher community suggests that both are important.

Shared beliefs at Mills derived in part from the founding process of the school. The consent decree tenets specified a general but nonetheless value-filled set of beliefs about education that teachers all agree to. In the "Participation" section, I describe how the Mills teacher community accommodates and transforms individuals who, in more typical schools, might be either marginalized or cast out entirely. It is important to note here, however, that in contrast to several theorists' suggestion that communities in their finest form are all-inclusive, Mills' teacher community had boundaries and an initial vision sufficiently clear to attract individuals who shared a basic set of beliefs. While there are many structures still in place to ensure that every individual participates in the life and shape of the community (witness the way each teacher was all but required to say something during the opening meeting in the cafeteria, for example), the founding principal made clear to potential teachers that if their educational philosophy was sufficiently different from the initial vision for the school, there were other schools in which they could teach.

Though no teacher from the original Mills was explicitly barred from applying, it is notable that so few chose to; and it is notable that the new staff—more diverse than most in age, ethnicity, gender, race, and sexual orientation—nonetheless came together around a particular vision defined in its most nascent form by the founding principal. Teachers described the staff that he hired as young, enthusiastic, idealistic, and often breaking away from other school settings where they did not feel supported for what they wanted to accomplish. Moreover, each teacher hired knew that joining Mills meant committing oneself to a mission, one likely to require long hours and involvement in many projects.

This initial sense of common purpose contributed not only to the professional culture that Mark and others describe and that is evident at faculty events, but also to a community orientation to curriculum, intertwining of individual classroom practices, and a collective responsibility for issues like scheduling, admissions, and discipline. In time, the base would expand to include shared beliefs derived specifically from collective experiences of the community as well as from individual experiences of members within the community. The initial shared beliefs served as a platform from which to formulate a school philosophy, though they do not adequately describe the system of shared beliefs at work among the faculty. These beliefs also emerge from structures and processes within the school. Mills has specific structures and processes in place encouraging the generation and evolution of a shared belief system that generally unites rather than divides the faculty. Despite some differences in philosophy, professional background, and teaching styles, the faculty emphasizes common ground when task-oriented projects must be done. Of course teachers at Mills also have beliefs that are not shared and even those that divide the faculty. These are discussed in the section "Dissent."

Conversations about curriculum like the one from the social studies department meeting described previously highlight the ways shared beliefs are identified and reinforced. Though the teachers are clearly starting from a general basis of agreement on what matters in education, there are

also formal structures in place that promote discussion around these beliefs. In coming together to develop a theme that runs through three grades
of social studies, teachers are organizing their work around the type of
communication that Dewey (1916) hopes for: communication that show-
cases similar "emotional and intellectual dispositions." Similarly, in the
opening meeting of the school year, each teacher's story about his or her
summer emphasized those aspects of the experiences that were most consistent with the philosophical commitments of the school as a whole.

The faculty's commitment to teaching students to think critically about
the social and political forces that act on their world results in the unfold-
ing and development of the teachers' own shared beliefs. One science
teacher reflected on the process of curriculum planning:

> A lot of the people here are very political. I think there's certainly a
> dominant political line, pretty liberal. . . . And I think that's signifi-
> cant, like when we plan Awareness Month activities, we know that
> if you're going to teach this stuff, the families have to talk about
> how you teach about racism, we have to discuss that among our-
> selves. Through planning for Awareness Month or [other interdisci-
> plinary curriculum units], because of the way we try to integrate the
> curriculum, our team [of the four teachers in the family] has had a
> lot of really intense discussions around big issues and have come to
> realize the ways we all agree on certain basic principles. (i03.29)

These discussions often lead to the rethinking of previously held beliefs
and, over time, contribute to a process of developing shared understandings and convictions that are always in flux. During a family meeting, a
sixth-grade teacher recalled the positive contribution made by a former
teacher who often challenged their beliefs:

> Does everyone remember Rick with the flag burning incident? [lots
> of uh huhs]. You know, Rick really served a purpose, and it gets
> back to what Doris was saying I think, that he was the Devil's
> advocate. He stood up and he would say things and poke people
> and irritate people but also made people talk sometimes, and think
> about what was important to us. (sb6)

In this way, teachers' beliefs about both purposes of school and strategies for teaching are the subject of discussion within the community and
are reshaped and refined on an ongoing basis.

Mills teachers' shared commitments are put into practice through a
variety of collective planning activities, staff development activities, and

special projects. How teachers participate in these activities and are recognized for their contributions to the community is the subject of the next section.

PARTICIPATION

I remember overhearing the following conversation between two teachers in the halls of the New York school where I taught sixth, seventh, and eighth graders:

Teacher #1: Were you at the meeting on Monday when we talked about next year?
Teacher #2: I can't remember. Was I?
Teacher #1: I can't remember either. I think you were. You were sitting next to Elena, weren't you?
Teacher #2: Oh yeah, why? Did we decide something?

Although Woody Allen once remarked that 90 percent of life is simply showing up, there is more to community participation than making an appearance. At Mills, teachers are highly involved in professional activities within the school, debating and making decisions about curriculum, budgets, and strategies and planning collective projects and schoolwide events. There is a strong ethos of participation.

How Does Participation Happen?

How do teacher professional communities encourage participation, especially in a culture and a profession that often emphasize passivity and isolation (Lieberman & Miller, 1984; Little, 1990; Lortie, 1975)? "Community life does not organize itself in an enduring way purely spontaneously," writes Dewey (1938); "it requires thought and planning ahead" (p. 56). At Mills, teacher participation in the life of the community takes many and varied forms. The common thread is an explicit attention to "planned inclusivity" (rather than the "allowed for" or passive inclusivity found at Brandeis). The result is *legitimate participation* by most members of the community.

Henry Giroux (1988) uses the term *legitimate participation* to describe forms of democratic participation that are public and that have effects (p. 217). Similarly, Benjamin Barber (1984) argues that democratic participation requires not only laws to enable voting and participation, but also strategies to encourage it. Enabling participation, Barber notes, is procedural democracy, within which members of the community maintain the right to vote; that is distinct from a participatory democracy in which members of the community exercise that right. At Mills, planned inclusivity results in high faculty participation in decision making in which members of the faculty community not only have the right to participate but also employ that right.

To promote participation, the Mills faculty balances institutionalized structures with room for innovation. Participation is highly structured during various activities and stages of evolution of the Mills teacher community. When the staff decided to reorganize the school into six families each comprised of the four subject area teachers, participation and interaction did not magically or "naturally" occur. As one teacher explained:

> When our family was first put together [in the spring of 1989], we didn't know each other at all. Jeremy was teaching in the other building, Donna was teaching down the hall but we had hardly interacted at all and Lisa was in two different classrooms. It was announced that we were to work on these teams together, and I looked at everybody on the team and I thought, "I don't even know who these people are." So we were asked to begin to talk to each other and see how things might work. . . . It was very busy. It was May and because we were all eighth-grade teachers, there's all the graduation stuff that happens at the end of the year. We made a couple of attempts and it didn't happen, it just didn't happen. Finally Carlos [the principal at the time] says, "Okay, why aren't you people meeting?" He finally gave us this mandate that we had to at least talk to each other and see what kinds of things we could come together on. He gave us assignments! It was really hard because at that time it felt very artificial to just be thrown together with people that I didn't know at all. (i01.29)

Recall the opening meeting of the year in which virtually every teacher related a story about his or her summer. Starting on one side of the room and continuing to the other, teachers were required to actively "pass" if they did not want to talk rather than signal their intent if they did.

Used often in many faculty meetings and staff development, structured narrative or storytelling (stories from their own experiences) creates not only a means for hearing voices that otherwise might be unheard but also connects the Mills faculty to the experiences of its members, creating an important interaction between the local school community and the larger global communities beyond the school. This can be seen in teachers' tales of summer events and experiences in other communities. Sabrina and

Pasqual participated in the Connections program. Donna and four other Mills teachers attended a workshop on portfolios. Raquel "got reacquainted" with her daughter. Almost every teacher shared stories and events and in the process established a connection to the other teachers. Teachers' stories or narratives are also a means for establishing identities as individuals (who have experiences outside of the community). By connecting individual experience within and outside of the community, participation contributes to the formation of individual identities in relation to the other members of the community.

Planned inclusivity of this sort leads to norms of participation that outlive the artificial structures. "At that time it felt very artificial to just be thrown together with people that I didn't know at all," recalled the teacher I quoted above. The four teachers in this family—the one together the longest at Mills—now meet twice a week from 1:30 to 3:00 P.M. and often schedule additional meeting times when needed. On Mondays they "staff" (bring all of their perspectives on an individual student together in an effort to solve potential problems), and on Tuesdays they discuss curriculum. Witness a typical Tuesday meeting of this family more than three years after Carlos, the former principal, gave the teachers "assignments" to meet in an effort to catalyze regular meetings.

The Family Meeting

As Lena and Donna arrive in Lisa's classroom, the wall-mounted telephone is ringing. Lena answers the phone.

"Lisa's not here, but she'll be back soon," she says as Donna sits down at one of a cluster of five desks arranged near the door. "Yes, she'll be back. Our family meeting starts in five minutes." Lena writes a note on Lisa's desk. Lena, Donna, Lisa, and Jeremy are, respectively, the language arts, social studies, science, and math teachers for this eighth-grade family.

Jeremy, who did not attend the late summer teacher planning days, pokes his head in the door and asks with a grin "Do we have a meeting?" Lena and Donna ignore the rhetorical question. Jeremy comes in and sits down at the desk nearest the door and furthest from Donna. He takes out a crossword puzzle.

Lena sits down across from Donna and begins to tell the others about her fitful sleep, tossing and turning, thinking about Kara, the eighth-grade student whose parent conference took place at yesterday's meeting. "In my 15 years of teaching, I've never seen anything like that. That girl just didn't know how to keep it together, and her parents certainly weren't any help. I just can't believe what some of these kids endure. I kept repeating to myself—in my dream!—tenet number eight, tenet number eight." The eighth tenet or belief statement comes up for discussion repeatedly at faculty gatherings ("If individuals do not learn, then those assigned to be their teachers should accept responsibility for this failure and should take appropriate remedial action").

Lisa comes in carrying a pile of papers, which she deposits on her desk. "I want to show you all something. Marlin wrote all these gang-related words on the desk during third period." They all read the desk. "I just wanted you all to know." They reconfirm the conference date with Marlin and his parents that they had decided on yesterday. Lena remarks that in addition to their family's learning challenge on violence, Marlin will probably benefit from Awareness Month activities. "'Faggot' isn't necessarily gang-related," Lena says.

Today's curriculum meeting begins with a brief discussion about parents' "Back to School" night the following week. "We need to sensitize parents," notes Lena, "to the fact that our eighth-grade curriculum deals with lots of heavy topics." She cites as examples African-American history and racism, Native American history, and Anti-Semitism. Jeremy begins a different topic when Donna cuts in, reminding the group that they need an agenda for the meeting. They decide with the time remaining that they should discuss Awareness Month curriculum and schedule Native American Day.

Lisa reports that she is working with a local group called Community United Against Violence to make connections between her science curriculum unit on the family and the family's current Awareness Month work.

"A lot of these kids bring stuff that's going on in their families to school with them," Donna points out. "It would be great if we can give them a forum to look at some of that smartly, in their classes."

Lena, the language arts teacher, is next. She is using Eli Wiesel's Night for her Awareness Month unit on the Holocaust. "I decided to start with literature rather than other stuff, so I can cover Awareness Month issues, but also do literature. I brought a lot of vocabulary in, like Lisa had on her board yesterday."

Jeremy begins, "As you know, my Awareness Month is really awareness week, because [he pauses] I don't know more than that." The others smile as Jeremy continues. "I'm having them look at the word *ethnicity*—how it derived from the word *ethic*."

Donna explains her social studies focus on discrimination and explains that she will have her students examine the current bills before the California legislature on immigration. "How do we know things aren't just your personal experience," she adds, "or if it's a wider issue of xenophobia?"

"What's xenophobia?" Jeremy asks.

Donna explains the fear of foreigners she believes is responsible for the spate of anti-immigration bills. "I'm also going to brainstorm with them things that were done in all their classes, so I'll try to have them pull it all together and say, 'How did I become more aware and what can I do with all of this?'"

As they begin to schedule Native American Day, Lisa interrupts. "You know the other thing I was thinking? Kids get so set in the mind set of you know this nation and our borders and our resources. Human beings, not just Americans, need these resources, and just the term 'immigrant' already starts us in this direction of fearing people who just want normal lives."

"Yeah, and then the other point could be that you get crowded cities and stuff. The whole issue of migration in California, you know people came where there were resources and there was the dustbowl," Donna adds.

Jeremy leans forward and asks "Well, has that happened in other places?"

Donna continues. "Sure, almost everywhere. I mean people migrate to where they can survive, like all the Irish immigrants came and soon there was all this anti-Irish sentiment."

"Uh huh."

"When there are enough resources," Donna continues, "it's all fine. But when there's not enough for everyone, that's what happens. And people get used to having certain standards, you know three cars, and it seems pretty OK to exclude whoever you want . . ."

Lena whispers to Lisa "I'm an internationalist, unless I have to claim Costa Rican descent." Lisa laughs. "At least I really think we can't just ignore certain segments of our population and pretend that everyone's a part of things."

"We do need to schedule this stuff," Donna reminds the other teachers, now wholly entrenched in a conversation about nationhood and borders.

Most Mills teachers contribute to the community far beyond their contractually required classroom duties. In this family meeting, all four teachers engaged in discussion on curriculum practices, strategies, and principles of education. Most notably, the topic of discussion reflects the norms of participation for the group. Here is what separates Mills teachers from the unfulfilled rhetoric of community found in so many other schools: Notions of inclusivity ("We can't just ignore certain segments of our population") and participation are inseparable from the process by which the faculty engage in their meeting.

Jeremy, who does not share all the same political commitments of his colleagues, nonetheless participates in the discussion. Unlike Brandeis, where teachers are given the opportunity to participate but often choose not to, Mills teachers are rarely silent. The catalyzing influence of past events on participation, however, does little to explain the influence of norms of participation on teachers new to the community. In what follows, I discuss two interrelated features of community maintenance: the experience of new members and the historicity of the community.

Introducing New Teachers to the Participatory Culture

The climate of participation at Mills absorbs newcomers (ob52–53). Interviews with teachers new to the Mills faculty reveal that, during the back-to-school meeting and the two days of faculty-planned activities that followed, they felt drawn in to a general climate of contribution and expression (i10.4; ob12). "At first I felt sort of isolated," the new seventh-grade math teacher told me,

> just sort of watching [the veteran Mills teachers] deal with the schedule. I didn't really know what they were talking about . . . but it didn't take me long to realize that, here, everyone seems to have something to contribute and everyone gets a chance to say what they have to, and people are fine about disagreement in our family, there's plenty of it. (i10.8)

Another teacher had taught at three different schools and now believes she has found the place she would like to stay:

> I'm a hard worker and I was getting tired of doing a lot of things and being looked at as a person who was tooting their horn instead of a person who was just doing their job. I feel like I'm finally around people who work hard. I feel really comfortable here. (i01.5)

The realization that not only are teachers' contributions to the community common but also that they are recognized was a powerful one for some teachers. Several, like the following teacher, reported that the recognition seemed "authentic" rather than ceremonial.

> My first year here, I noticed right away that at the consent decree days that we had at the beginning [of the year], people applauded each other. People recognized each other, whether their contribution was getting the dessert or making contact with parents about this or that or planning the schedule. Whatever it was, everyone was appreciative. At my experience at faculty meetings before, it's been like everyone just wants to get out of there. (i10.8)

This process of participation and recognition allows new teachers to break with their own expectations of teacher professional communities derived from past experiences or from their own notions of professional life in schools. Consequently, many teachers are aware of the differences between Mills' professional ethos and that of other schools in which they had taught. Lena, the eighth-grade language arts teacher, for example, remembers her old school and first coming to Mills:

> What [teachers at school where I used to teach] were doing now was what they were going to continue to do. No change. No growth. I remember that every time I tried to do something extra, something new, I got the message loud and clear from people: "Chacon," they would say, "this is how we've always done it here." And that was that. Everyone was very suspicious of anything that wasn't the usual program. There was no rocking the boat. Now when I came here, it was like having a blank page to start from. There was a sense of real empowerment, like this was a place where you could try new things, actually, where you couldn't help *but* try new things. (i01.29)

One of the ways the ethos of participation is conveyed to new teachers is through the exploration and celebration of the community's history.

History and Historicity

The evolution of events over time gives every community a history. Examining this history provides a sense of the community's evolution—the ways events unfolded and their effects. It also creates what Bellah and his colleagues (1985) call a "community of memory," influenced by its past and the memories of significant or legendary events. Most importantly, incorporating the community's history in the service of the community ethos provides an opportunity for newcomers to be inculcated into the culture of participation and interaction and for veterans to celebrate it.

One of the ways history is acknowledged in the Mills community is demonstrated by a staff activity that took place early in the year. For a staff development day, Mark, Sara, and Lena planned a time-line activity. They split the entire staff into groups based on the years they first came to Mills, starting in 1983, the first year after the consent decree took effect, and continuing in two-year increments to the present. The groups recalled significant activities and events that happened during their starting years and wrote them down on butcher-block paper. Each group then gave a two- to three-minute presentation about these events to the entire staff.

The first group of teachers, those who had been at Mills the longest, spoke of their initial sense of purpose after coming together as a new staff. They recalled the "feelings of possibility" as well as the "tensions and expectations" of the design years. Several other groups chose to perform a skit or sing a song portraying historic moments.

> "We need a vision. We need a vision." The group that has called themselves "The Crying Game Years" walks in a line across the front of the room, snapping and chanting. "We need a vision. We need a vision."
>
> "Can we begin the faculty meeting, please?" the teacher playing the role of principal at the time of restructuring asks. Then he sobs. "If you teachers aren't willing to undertake the risk to restructure the school for these kids, I don't want to be your principal anymore." More sobs. "I mean it." The audience shrieks with laughter.
>
> The spokesperson of the performers explains that when teachers began to balk at the dramatic changes that had been discussed and formulated by the whole staff, such as block scheduling and an emphasis on interdisciplinary curriculum, the principal, who "had a strong vision of the way the school should go," actually began to cry at a faculty meeting. After elaborating on a few other memories from their first years, the line of teachers exits once again snapping and chanting "We got a vision, we got a vision."

This legendary event in the history of the school was referred to in faculty meetings and was recognizable (in interviews) by teachers who had been at the school only a few weeks. In addition, the laughter, the enthusiasm, and the spirit of performance conveyed an atmosphere in which everyone could take part in the proceedings. In fact, the activity was deliberately planned to draw in those teachers who might otherwise sit on the sidelines. The planners recalled the strategy:

> We wanted to include everybody, and it was planned with that in mind, to allow nobody to cop out or just sit around. That was very important. So when people put on the skits, everybody did them. No one was allowed to sit back. . . . 'Cause Jeremy, heavens he will sit back for days. He will sort of sneak out the door. No, he had to be actively engaged. Everybody did. (i07.2)

Another group performed a skit portraying the years following the faculty decision to divide the school into interdisciplinary teams of teachers and students called families. After the skit, several teachers spoke to the other faculty about their experience:

> This was a very sensitive year for us coming in. It was very hard for some of us coming into a situation with families already set up and one or two people were just plopped into bad situations. (sb7)

> The first year that we had families, we had very different experiences. I found that they were tremendously supportive; but not everybody was really encompassed into a formal family, and some of the families didn't work out, so we were trying to point that out [in the skit]. (sb8)

By emphasizing some of the tensions that emerged during the process of creating the family system, this group conveyed to newcomers the sense of flux that is critical to the growth of the community.

> [Even as] the families got better and better, we also became six separate little worlds, and now we have less and less time to interact with each other. (ob12)

This last quotation provoked a discussion about the tensions between the time spent within the families and the time spent together as an entire faculty and school. Mark suggested the discussion continue at a faculty meeting so the in-service day could stay on schedule.

By exploring the collective history of the community and sharing legends and stories, teachers create and maintain a community ethos. Newcomers are drawn in not only by becoming privy to this history but also by the participatory process by which the history is presented, reflected on, and critically examined. "Just seeing everybody and realizing 'Wow, when they came here, there were different problems,'" a teacher observed as she watched the skits about Mills' history, "and they got past it. I can just see how everybody was engaged, everybody was really listening" (ob92).

INTERDEPENDENCE

Social theorists have long pointed to the importance of activities that require and nourish interdependence in building meaningful connections among individuals (Hirschi, 1969; Scherer, 1972). When people are engaged with others in worthwhile projects that draw on their abilities, relationships form. The resulting intertwining of individual and collective activity—of interdependence through participation in shared practices—is often cited as one of the component features of community. To Bellah and his colleagues (1985), for example,

> a community is a group of people who are socially interdependent, who participate together in discussion and decision making, and who share certain practices that both define the community and are nurtured by it. (p. 333)

Teachers in schools are no different and yet teaching is so often a solitary endeavor. In contrast to the norms of autonomy and privacy that typify the culture of teaching in so many schools (Little, 1990; Lortie, 1975; Metz, 1986; Shulman, 1989), the Mills faculty is characterized by a sense of collective work and activity in which individual teachers rely on one another's efforts.

There are many ways that the Mills faculty depend on one another during day-to-day practices and there are formal and informal structures in place to facilitate collective practice and responsibility. In the previous section on participation, we saw how teachers come together to make decisions in faculty meetings, how new teachers are inculcated into a participatory culture, how the faculty critically (and with humor) explore their history together, and how the space for participation is created even for those who might otherwise remain marginal to community activities. Redesigning the school as described earlier (establishing a vision; creating mission statements; formulating policies, schedules, and practice) also is an example of and contributes to a sense of mutual need and obligation within the faculty. In this section, I focus on curriculum design and implementation and the ways these activities both require and foster interdependence in the Mills teacher community. Because interdependence is woven into virtually every facet of complex curricula, this section is significantly longer than other sections in this chapter.

How is interdependence fostered in the Mills teacher community? John Dewey and others have pointed to the importance of engaging students in more "natural" activities that are social, participatory, and relevant (Bowman, 1984; Cohen, 1994; Dewey, 1938; Wigginton, 1985). The same might be said to apply to teachers. As the Mills faculty and staff plan and implement curriculum, they also engage in the types of professional and social interaction that reformers seek to promote. In department meetings, teachers discuss in depth their curricular goals, innovations, and tie-ins to the California state framework for their discipline. They also deliberate on possible connections to other disciplines. In grade-level meetings, teachers coordinate between the disciplines and consider assessment strategies. In faculty meetings, teachers and staff ponder schoolwide curriculum events. And the members of the volunteer Curriculum Committee discuss overarching schoolwide learning goals, strategies, and philosophies, and plan curriculum for in-house staff development (such as the in-service day described earlier). That curriculum development is a collective enterprise is evident in almost every aspect of teaching and learning.

All of these events are examples of professional and social interdependence. Following Dewey (1938), I will call these communally interdependent tasks "collective projects." Curriculum design and implementation at Mills is a collective project that draws on the talents and abilities of individual teachers and creates conditions under which collective as well as solitary practice builds and relies on interdependence.

Interdependence in Planning:
The Learning Challenge Curriculum

The most explicitly community-oriented curriculum activity at Mills is the learning challenge. Learning challenges at Mills are built on the model provided by the local division of Project 2061, a national science-based curriculum initiative named for the next appearance of Halley's comet—a reminder that curriculum reform is a slow and steady process. Each challenge consists of "a worthy task that engages the students in investigating and responding to issues (challenges of belief), in solving problems (challenges to action), in designing and creating products and performances (challenges to imagination), and/or inquiring into why and how specific explanations of how the world works have come to be trusted (challenges to curiosity and skepticism)" (Fargas, 1993, p. 3).

Each family of four teachers at Mills comes together early in the year to choose a "prompting challenge" around which they can develop an interdisciplinary curriculum unit. The units range in length from one week to six weeks and are designed to engage students in social issues and problems of local concern in a way that "organically" draws on each of the disciplines. Once a topic is chosen, other teachers and staff in the school are encouraged to join with a challenge group that interests them. This serves to interweave the work of a larger group of teachers within the school as well as to reduce class size for the duration of the challenge. These teachers and staff become what Mills teachers affectionately call an "extended family" and coordinate virtually all of their individual classes together, linking teachers' work as well as reducing class size for the duration of the challenge. Both traditionally academic classes and electives focus on subjects that inform the creation of various final products for the challenge.

Several Thursday and Friday in-service days (when students are not at school) throughout the year are devoted to the learning challenges, allowing teachers to reflect on and share their experiences from the previous year's challenges and formulate plans for the current year. Family 8-II chose violence as a theme for their challenge. The following takes place on the morning of the November in-service day as Donna, the 8-II social studies teacher, on her way to the meeting, pokes her head into the 8-II science teacher's classroom.

"Going over to the meeting, Lisa?"

Lisa grabs a notebook and a few piles of learning challenges materials, and they walk toward the cafeteria together. They will be spending the day talking about violence, the subject of their challenge this year. In the hallway, they stroll past a student-made poster with a Frederick Douglass quotation. "If there is no struggle, there is no progress" is printed in block letters. "Power concedes nothing without a demand." When they enter the cafeteria at 9:15 A.M., the meeting is already under way.

The day's schedule is posted on an easel at the front of the room. Teachers and staff, each equipped with a large red three-ring binder, are slowly settling down to tables. After a quick consultation between Elissa, Mark, and Lena, the in-service day planners, the presentation and discussion of portfolio assessment is moved back one-half hour to accommodate a brief update on the state restructuring grant Mills received, Senate Bill 1274.

Today's Agenda

8:30–9:00	Informal networking. Pick up in-service folder on this table
9:00–9:15	Tom Connor Speaks!
9:15–10:00	Meet in last year's challenge groups
10:00–10:15	Break

10:15–12:15	Meet in cross-family groups
12:15–1:00	Lunch
1:00–2:00	Meet in extended families
2:00–2:45	Portfolio assessment sharing (Lloyd)
2:45–3:00	Announcements
3:00–3:05	Session evaluation

Though Elissa, a seventh-grade language arts teacher, points out the 2:45 time slot for announcements, she allows several early morning communiqués to slip in. Pasqual, a seventh-grade science teacher, announces that December 1 is World AIDS Day. "Four families are already attending the special assembly, and we can only accommodate four. Are there any loose fold-up chairs anywhere?" Another teacher asks Tom, the principal, to introduce the people she doesn't know at the meeting. Elissa responds to this request and introduces the new special education teacher, a visiting parent, and a student teacher.

By 9:20, the teachers split into last year's challenge groups, comprised of the "extended family." This includes the teachers of the four subject areas (math, science, language arts, and social studies) as well as other teachers and staff who worked with them on a particular challenge unit. These might include the art teacher, a physical education teacher, a counselor, custodial staff, and student teachers. The 8-II extended family group has ten people. As Donna sits down next to Jeremy, Jeremy asks her where she got the red folder.

"Oh, you are such a loser!" They both laugh. "They're from last year, Jeremy."

"Yeah, I couldn't find it," Jeremy replies sheepishly. As a math teacher, Jeremy isn't always sure that he can mold his curriculum to fit the challenges, which tend to be geared toward current issues in social studies. He occasionally does crossword puzzles during these meetings and today he has brought two.

Donna and Lena lead this group, explaining that each person here will have to tell other faculty and staff about last year's challenge. "Our task is to prepare a report for the mixed groups," Donna says. She turns to Jeremy and adds, "You will have 15 minutes to explain our challenge, like the criteria for assessment, why it's meaningful, how it matches the framework in your subject area, things like that." Jeremy looks concerned.

As Donna continues the explanation to the group, Lena speaks quietly to Jeremy. "Like a jigsaw," she explains. The group pours over the guiding questions that Elissa and Mark handed out. Discussion moves quickly.

"Well, under 'Quality Output' I would like to talk about improving our challenge," says Sharon, the computer resource aide, as she reads over the guiding questions.

"Yeah, we should start by trying to get a handle on number three: How did our challenge help to move toward whole school outcomes?" Donna reads.

"Students will be able to manage complex problems," Lena suggests, "address real-world issues, and take responsibility for themselves and their communities."

"Intuitively, we say this moved them along toward that," Donna adds, "but we have nothing to show what kinds of values developed or what—"

"We didn't identify tools to measure that," the computer resource teacher interrupts.

"How could you measure that other than just observing?" Lisa wonders out loud.

Jeremy, who had been grading math homework momentarily, switches to taking notes about what he will have to report to the mixed groups. "The students had observation notebooks," Jeremy pipes in, "but I think we need better forms of assessment."

By the end of the day, eighth-grade family II had decided that they would stay with the same prompting challenge they had used the year before, but modify some of the curriculum. The prompting challenge was in the form of a question: "How can you empower yourself and your peers to address the violence in your life and in society in a positive way?"

For the week preceding family 8-II's designated challenge week, students went to their classes on the regular schedule. Each teacher focused on skills and knowledge that they would utilize during the upcoming challenge. Lena, the language arts teacher, for example, had students write autobiographical accounts of incidents in which they or someone they knew were victims of violence. Exploring written representations of violence and autobiographical writing (Alice Walker's "Beauty When the Other Dancer Is the Self," for example), they generated ideas for addressing violence through writing. Jeremy, the math teacher, had students gather and analyze statistics on violence, while in social studies, Donna had them discuss notions of objectivity and subjectivity in news reporting.

At the end of the first week, students chose a mini-course that fell under the general theme of violence. For five entire days, students met in these groups to explore their "sub-challenge." Donna's group examined violence in the media; Lena's looked at gang violence; Jeremy's group explored the cost of violence in California, while Lisa led a group that looked at violence in families and relationships. The physical education teacher who joined their challenge group led students interested in the connections between violence in professional sports and in the larger society.

Though most learning challenges follow this mini-course model, one sixth-grade family's learning challenge ran for seven weeks with one day per week devoted to the challenge. In this challenge, Eran, Raquel, Elayne, and Doris worked with their students to develop a self-sustaining garden and distribution network to support the hungry in their Bay Area city. During the in-service day, Eran talked in their extended family group about why the challenge seemed to work so well the previous year for their at-risk students.

"I understand that it seemed to work for kids who usually tune out when you get to the serious academic stuff," Paul, the computer resource teacher, tells Eran, "but, I'm curious why you think that is. What is it about this type of curriculum that draws those kids in?"

Eran answers excitedly. "It was real."

"Hands on?"

"Not just hands on, it was a real-life situation. Things in the garden were growing. Homeless organizations were contacting them. Newspaper blurbs piqued their interest . . . kids were asking us questions in the middle of the week about it, in all their classes, after school . . . it was real life, they were thinking about it."

At 10:25, Elissa tells everyone to switch into mixed-family groups. "They're marked on each table," she explains, "look for your name."

Settled in his group, Eran tells about his class assignment to write a proposal to a hypothetical presidential commission on world hunger. The group was impressed that students had generated the idea.

"It causes problems too," Eran points out. "We found it difficult to set up criteria and standards that went across these activities and to set specific learning goals because they were changing so fast and students were coming up with a lot of them. It wasn't an insurmountable task, but it was difficult." Eran's group continues to discuss this and other issues as do the five other groups in the increasingly noisy cafeteria. When the lunch break is called, it is more than 20 minutes before the last group actually breaks.

When the sixth-grade teachers began the implementation of their challenges, students conducted research on homelessness, world hunger, food distribution, and sustainable growth. They consulted libraries, homeless organizations, and community groups. Students learned about plant growth, soil content analysis, and derivations of formulas for calculating volume and weight. They constructed planting boxes, determined the placement of support beams, investigated possibilities for irrigation, and together transformed the unused roof of the three-story school building into an urban garden where students and teachers planted, cultivated, and harvested a variety of vegetables and fruits. An art class painted a mural on the stairwell leading up to the new roof garden while a strange rumor spread among students that the sixth grade was actually building a rooftop swimming pool that only they would be able to use. The second year this challenge was implemented, Eran contacted the renowned chef at a local upscale restaurant to cook a benefit dinner using the vegetables students grew in the garden. They raised funds for local homeless groups, and spent an additional two weeks investigating the best means for distributing the money they raised.

The value of both of these curriculum units (as well as those of the four other families) could be measured in innumerable ways. Students and teachers are engaged in hands-on learning that is authentic, problem-based, and engaging. These curriculum units would be first-class examples of a variety of curriculum reform efforts underway nationwide that emphasize active and relevant project-based learning. The value I focus on here, however, is the ways in which planning and implementing these units bring the faculty and staff of Mills together around meaningful work. While dozens of community-building reforms focus directly (in workshops, for example) on fostering better communication and coaxing teachers to talk about matters of pedagogy and teaching, these learning challenges engage teachers together, interdependently, in collective work that *demands* high levels of interaction, communication, and professional dialogue.

If the cafeteria were a middle-school classroom, it would score high on assessment of engagement. The staff development day is highly structured and meticulously planned. Mark circulates among the tables advising the group leaders that they have four more minutes. Huge butcher-block sheets of paper in each group are filled with writing from brainstorming. In the mixed groups where a representative from each family describes the family's challenge, Mark has assigned specific roles: a reporter who will summarize for the whole faculty what happened in their group, a recorder who will document the group's discussion, and a timekeeper.

Following a few more scheduling changes and toward the end of the day as teachers are tiring, each family briefly reports plans for the current year's learning challenges to the entire faculty and staff. Each reporter accepts the growing number of jokes, wisecracks, and other punchy interruptions that signal to all the near end of a long day of planning.

"In a new style that is short, concise and succinct," Lloyd begins, "our challenge—'Chinese Cultural Contributions'—will be set in March instead of May to avoid conflict with one of the eighth-grade families' challenges." In the past, Lloyd's family's challenge has been social science–driven, Lloyd adds. "We hope to make it more math and science-driven this year." After finishing his concise report, Lloyd tips the front of his baseball cap, returns to the computer, which he has wheeled over to his table, and continues typing notes of the proceedings, a task he has taken on himself and has been devoted to the entire day.

Raquel reports that family 6-I will repeat the hunger garden and will include a group of the special education teacher's students. "We are going to request eight days of sub[stitute] time, ten hours planning time for four teachers and one para[professional] to work with us." She adds that as a second challenge this year, they are proposing the topic of city planning and community design.

Walter reports for the music department, which this year decided to do its own challenge rather than integrate into each family's challenge. "Putting on a concert is enough challenge for us," Walter says softly. As has become de rigueur when Walter speaks, several teachers yell "Can't hear you!" Donna, in a half-mumble, says, "The challenge is going to be hearing Walter talk." Everyone laughs.

Lena stands up for family 8-II. She has a smirk on her face that betrays impending antics. The previous year's learning challenges planning days were marked by some tension when 8-I accused family 8-II of "stealing" their challenge idea on violence. "Our planning was really easy," Lena announces. "We are going to do whatever 8-I is doing." Lena sits down and laughter fills the room. When it is quiet, Lena returns to her standing position and explains some modifications in their challenge.

The resource teacher for students with limited English skills announces that his students will be doing a small challenge [light applause]. "I want to let you know that they will be asking some of you if they can interview you in English," he explains, "and they have been told not to go to Spanish-speaking faculty, because the teachers may understand them."

"God Forbid!" someone yells followed by laughter.

Before the meeting draws to a close, Donna suggests that they change the following Wednesday's schedule to a Friday schedule since they have missed two Fridays for staff development days. Elissa asks if they should vote.

"Anyone opposed? . . . No? . . . Sold to the highest bidder."

"Thank you Elissa and Sara and Mark for an incredible amount of work," Donna announces as everyone applauds, "and to Mr. Connor [the principal] for the refreshments."

"Now we all know what folks did last year for their challenges and what they're thinking about for this year, and that's great" Connor says to continuing applause.

Donna leans over to Eran, who lives near her. "Want a ride?"

While learning challenges bring teachers together around the same task, other curriculum development endeavors also reflect a general emphasis on interdisciplinarity and therefore interdependence among the faculty. One of the monthly meetings of all the humanities teachers, for example, was devoted specifically to the integration of math in the humanities curriculum. Their discussion produced a range of integration ideas. Walter, the music teacher, suggested a unit on music and fractions, noting that at the end of each musical measure, the beats, which are represented as fractions of a whole, have to add up. A language arts teacher pointed out that poetry also draws on rhythm and fractions. "Iambic pentameter has both mathematical and poetic meaning." The learning disability resource teacher argued the importance of teaching mathematical and logical thinking. Donna and two other social studies teachers made a case for moving beyond the use of statistics as a way to integrate math. They talked about the book *How to Lie with Statistics* as a basis for exploring mathematical objectivity and subjectivity, truth and opinion, not just reporting the results of a survey. "Something like geography and longitude and latitude clearly draw on math," Donna suggested,

But I think numbers can do more than measure physical things. Any linear, logical thinking is mathematical. To be a good historian, you need to know what other questions need to be asked, even mathematical ones. We really need to raise our consciousness of what's possible . . . and that can start with meeting more often with humanities and math teachers. (sb137)

The commitment to interdisciplinary curriculum not only serves to unite the faculty around a shared philosophy of pedagogy and learning, but also provides opportunities for interaction, professional dialogue, and the sharing of individual practice. As another opportunity for collective work, meetings that seek to overlap curriculum also break down barriers between disciplines, between classrooms, and ultimately between individual teachers.

The tasks described are all notable for their relevance to the primary goal of teaching. The opportunities for interaction among teachers are structured around real tasks that must be accomplished rather than on social meetings designed to directly address issues of community. Relevance, however, is not always enough to bring people working on a collective project together. There must also be a shared base of experience and a shared outlook. The challenges exemplify this as well. Coming together around a project in which there is a common base of shared values and a common understanding of desirable pedagogy (project-based learning, for example) unites teachers and makes clear opportunities for building shared experiences.

Interdependence in Teaching

As students rush through the hallways after lunch, Donna and Lena run into each other. "I used that story about colonizing Mars today, and it worked beautifully!" Donna exclaims delightedly. Her social studies class is in the middle of a unit on colonialism. "You know what Raisha said?" Donna continues.

Lena shrugs her shoulders.

Donna imitates the eighth grader. "She said 'I'd worry about that. What if everyone started rounding people up who they didn't agree with, like they did to the witches, and put them in colonies on Mars?'"

Lena raises her eyebrows in approval. Lena's class is reading *The Crucible*. Her students have been doing projects on witch colonies and talking about the connections to contemporary intolerance of individuals who do not easily fit into mainstream America. Lena moves her hands in an upward spiral as if tracing an invisible DNA helix in a gesture that illustrates the way they are drifting in and out of each other's classroom curriculum. "They'll get it all eventually," Lena declares.

"From all sides," Donna adds as they both disappear into
their respective classrooms surrounded by a sea of eighth graders.

In the sections on the school's history and on curriculum design, I described how the Mills faculty comes together around explicitly collective
undertakings. Designing the school virtually from scratch, starting with
only the consent decree tenets and a "blank piece of paper," engendered a
sense of common mission and required a great deal of interaction, communication, and the forging of a collective educational philosophy. Similarly, planning the challenge curriculum units across disciplines, and reflecting on and assessing them with the entire faculty and staff, served as
an example of teacher collaboration rare for its complexity and depth of
interdependence across disciplines. These types of collaboration reflect and
contribute to the sense of professional mission at Mills. In both examples,
teachers work together on tasks that require a great deal of time and energy and represent a common design goal. I focused on the actual planning time in which teachers work together, interacting both professionally
and socially.

The chance hallway encounter described above, however, signals another aspect of the common sense of mission among Mills teachers: the
breakdown of the traditionally solitary domain of the teacher's classroom.
The classroom may be the least likely place to manifest communal associations due to the constraints of teaching and the organization of schools.
At Mills, interdisciplinary and interdependent curriculum, a common sense
of mission that underlies the teaching of any particular subject area, and
the relationships among teachers conspire to create a sense of collective
practice even when teachers work alone.

Each family of four teachers (social studies, language arts, math, and
science) meets at least twice each week for one and a half hours. Time is
provided for these meetings by scheduling electives and physical education in a way that frees teachers within a given family for the same time
period. Most families use one of the weekly meetings to discuss any students having difficulties and the other to discuss curriculum. The planning
for the challenge units begins in the curriculum meetings and extends to
the larger staff development days.

The challenges exemplify the impact of collective planning on individual teachers' practice by placing classroom curriculum directly in the
service of a broader goal shared among the teachers of a given family.
During the eighth-grade family's challenge on violence described earlier,
each teacher was concerned not only with meeting the requirements of the
state framework in their subject area, but also with doing so through an

authentic collective project, in this case understanding and transforming the role of violence in their students' lives and in society.

The structured interdependence of individual teachers' lessons is built into the design of these units. In one curriculum meeting, for example, Lena, the language arts teacher, asked Jeremy, the math teacher,

> Jeremy, could you explain how you're doing the link between tax expenditures and violence in your statistics unit, because I'm trying to get them to look at all the different consequences of gang violence and maybe I could prepare them for what you're doing? (sb192)

Questions like this sprout from the deliberate planning of an interdisciplinary structure.

Lisa, the science teacher in the same eighth-grade family, described another, smaller challenge on energy and the effects of oil spills on oceans. They implemented this unit three years in a row:

> We all have very concrete valuable things we did for a whole week and they were completely integrated, and the kids wrote a common problem-solving essay that had to incorporate parts from all four classes. The kids were really engaged and we really saw things come in from all four classes. We're at the point now where we're refining it, and it's getting better every year. (i03.8)

Another teacher spoke of the same unit:

> The curriculum has a high interest for us and for the kids. It's one of the times that we hear kids raise their hand and say things like "Isn't that like such and such that I heard in Chacon's class?" or "I know the statistics for that." They're actively bringing information from one class to another and applying it which is really exciting when you see it. Each part builds one on the other. (i02.10)

The elements of Learning Challenges, by their design, result in overlap and interdependence.

Even curriculum not overtly interdisciplinary, however, results in significant interaction and communication. Vocabulary used in Lisa's science unit on "nature versus nurture" controversies sprang up three days later in Lena's writing assignment on discrimination and the following week in Donna's lesson on immigration. When teachers include words like *xeno-*

phobia and *homophobia* in their respective lessons, they engender implicit connections and link disciplines for both students and teachers.

In another example of the ways individual classroom practices become interconnected in this eighth-grade family, Lena and her students were trying to think of another word for "partner." "What is a word that Ms. Clark taught you that fits with that?" Lena asked.

"Ally!" two students answer simultaneously, recalling the science teacher's lesson on parasitic and synergistic relationships occurring in nature.

"Ally, right. Ally."

Donna, the social studies teacher, follows a lesson on Native American history in which students explore tribes living on the plains by pointing out that students will be learning about the plains biome[2] in science two weeks later.

The curriculum meetings (as well as bi-monthly department meetings) provide teachers with simple knowledge of each other's classroom lessons, even when there is no explicit effort to coordinate curricular content. When, in the middle of a class in which students are creating poster presentations, a teacher phones the art teacher and asks whether students can come during lunch to work on their projects, the art teacher already knows what the project is and suggests various artistic media that might fit the needs of the presentation and also utilize the students' current work in art class; the computer resource teacher knows a great deal about each teacher's class project so that he can offer students assistance that goes beyond technical help. Some of this knowledge comes directly from formal curriculum meetings, but some arises spontaneously because of teachers' lunchtime conversations, hallway conversations, faculty meetings, department meetings, and staff development days.

All of these exchanges reflect an ethic in which each teacher's curriculum is part of a larger collective mission. One teacher told me about her experience reading her class' student journals:

> I was having them write about how things were going after three and a half weeks of eighth grade. A lot of the kids were writing that the teachers really care about kids in this family and things like "we really like that you guys are helping us" and "we feel like 8th grade is gonna be hard but that there's people here to help us." All that kind of stuff and I thought to myself "They aren't saying you Ms. Chacon, they are saying the teachers in 8-II [Ms. Chacon's family]." (i01.8)

---

2. Biome is the ecological term for all organisms living within a single ecological region.

Ms. Chacon spent the weekend reading the journals and spoke about how despite the fact that this was an assignment given in her class, for her class only, it made her work as a classroom teacher feel part of something larger.

> I had this overwhelming sense of connectedness and positiveness about my students' first few weeks in 8-II—connectedness with the teachers, with the sense of what we're trying to get at. Of course we disagree on stuff, but I don't think our kids really see as much of our dissension as the things we all care about. (i01.8)

Mills teachers' collective sense of responsibility for student learning affects not only the experience of learning for students but also the experience of teaching for teachers. In the next section I describe the impact on what is every teacher's most difficult and frustrating preoccupation.

Collective Responsibility for Discipline

> In Eran's sixth-grade social studies class, which immediately follows lunch, students are having trouble working quietly. After 15 minutes of disruptions, Eran begins a sermon familiar to every middle-school teacher. "Sit down at your desks! I've had it with all of you. If you can't be trusted to work on these projects with respect for your peers and for me, then we won't work on them! You guys are on probation. And I'm disappointed." The remainder of the class is without major disruptions, but is nonetheless frustrating for Eran (i05.41).
>
> The students are scheduled to go to Elayne's language arts class next, and as Eran lines them up to leave, Elayne appears in the hallway.
>
> "What is going on?" she asks Eran within earshot of the students. Eran and Elayne discuss what happened and by the time the bell rings, the students are quiet and pensive. Eran and Elayne remain in the doorway, talking.
>
> Five minutes later, Elayne begins her class in the next room. "This is unacceptable. If you can't do this kind of work, there are other schools." She speaks in measured tones, quiet but forceful and serious. "If you're going to act like this, we won't do creative stuff . . . we can all give you worksheets. I heard you all coming in saying, 'Boy was he mad' and 'Isn't he angry?' Well of course he's angry. He worked hard to plan something for you today. And so have I." Eran enters the room during what is now his free period and sits at Elayne's desk, listening.

There are many case studies that describe in painful detail the demoralizing effects on teachers of isolation when a classroom gets out of control (Kidder, 1989; Lightfoot, 1983; Sizer, 1984, 1992). Classroom management and discipline problems are an inevitable part of every teacher's work, and Mills is no exception. What is different is the perspective teachers are able to maintain as adults even when faced with the disapproval of 30 teenagers. While teachers generally have no choice but to rely on students for their own sense of professional identity and self-worth (Meier, 1995; Varenne, 1983), at Mills, discipline problems become a collective responsibility. Because teachers talk extensively about students at weekly meetings and interact on a daily basis in each other's classrooms and hallways, often daunting matters like discipline become a collective concern. Teachers support one another. One teacher, who started her teaching career at Mills, recalls her first year:

> Thinking back to my very first year, and I was a brand new teacher, I took over from another teacher. And I was completely overwhelmed. I remember Pasqual, who was the science teacher right down the hall at that point from me, being extremely supportive. When we would go off to plan our own part of some curriculum, he would share ideas and share lessons and let me cry on his shoulder. [It was] a time when I felt as if I had no classroom management and the kids were really wild and saying really rude things. And I felt very incompetent. I think I remember at the end of the day, coming out of the classroom in tears. He would reassure me that it had been the same for him. He would always check-in, too, every day or every couple days. "How did it go?" "How are things going?" "Do you need some help?" (i03.9-10)

The relationships among teachers also provide "real-time" support during actual moments of classroom disruption. The same teacher continued describing the support she received from Pasqual:

> I also remember him coming into my classroom during class sometimes and joking with me about a group of students who were testing me all the time . . . there was something about them seeing us, the adults, being above their nonsense, that made me feel more competent . . . it let me laugh off the whole thing even though I knew I had a lot to learn about classroom management. (i03.11-12)

Not only are teachers supported in this way, thereby diminishing the possibility of teacher "burnout," which so often derives directly from fatigue over classroom management issues, but the impact on managing the discipline problems themselves is worth mentioning. Students, in witnessing this type of unity among teachers, are less likely to challenge teachers. "Don't let them know they're getting to you" is popular advice for new teachers. In the incident involving Eran's class described above, students continued to voice what they saw as legitimate concerns, but refrained from the type of group-act that can so easily spiral out of control, leaving adult teachers all too vulnerable to the—at times sincere, but often immature— perspective of children.

Not all teachers at Mills, however, experience the sense of support described above. When ideas about how children should be disciplined differed (which they did for a few teachers), the more common sense of isolation replaces support.

> There's real differences of opinion here about setting standards for students. There's real differences of opinion here about discipline. There's real differences of opinion in how much students can and should be allowed to be involved in setting the agenda for the school and be responsible for their behavior. . . . It makes me wonder if I'm the only teacher who thinks this way. (i05.9)

> I think some teachers just don't deal with at-risk students in the way I do. They just fail them. And they don't go to the dances. . . . We have some difference in philosophy. I don't think grades should be something you use as discipline. It's an issue that divides us in some ways. (i07.2)

The teachers who believed their philosophy on discipline was quite different from the faculty majority nonetheless reported a general sense of support stemming from broader shared beliefs.

> When I see members of Mills out with other teachers in the district, I see how we're similar. But in the school itself, we feel very different sometimes. Things like the control of students in the hallway. I mean that seems like a big difference. But then when I go to visit another school or something, I see how similar the Mills teachers are. We all share some basic beliefs about the world and about teaching. (i08.22)

Those views that are shared and those that are not are grist for what is arguably the most interesting set of emerging issues in the studies of school communities, and this brings me to the fourth feature of community described by social theorists: concern for dissenting minority opinions.

DISSENT

While shared beliefs unite most Mills teachers in a common sense of mission, they periodically alienate others. Recall that the Brandeis faculty community is characterized by a quest for professional coexistence and tolerance of different educational philosophies and strategies. Brandeis teachers allow a range of beliefs and practices, but this range is also quite bounded. Faculty with outspoken beliefs that stray far from mainstream, liberal educational philosophy and politics are discouraged from teaching those views. The rhetoric of the Brandeis teacher community, however, is the rhetoric of liberalism and tolerance. The Mills faculty community, on the other hand, is characterized by deliberately intertwined practices and shared purposes. Intertwined practice, then, results in many more opportunities for conflict. Mark described this phenomenon as follows:

> What do you do when conflict emerges or when you have a weak teacher? I've taught in schools where you can kind of hide it because everyone's doing their own thing. But when you're in a family, you can't hide. You can't disguise it, it comes out. It has to be dealt with. We need to be really closely aligned in our curriculum, in policies about parent involvement, about discipline, about all of the issues that go into this. And it had to be by consensus and not everybody could really agree. Before [restructuring] people could kind of keep quiet and it really didn't matter at the school level. (i12.22)

Conflict within the Mills teacher community is dealt with more openly than not; and teachers participate in meaningful dialogue and in decision making in numbers far greater than in many schools. While this can be attributed at least in part to explicit mechanisms for participation and conflict resolution, the fact that the faculty share common commitments to working together toward similar ends cannot be ignored. Recall that, in contrast to Brandeis in which only two Bayland district teachers were turned away by the hiring committee, a vast majority of Mills' 40 teachers resigned and the rehiring process was based on clearly stated goals and values. Indeed, in the last seven years, two teachers left Mills to transfer to another school, and many teachers now at Mills believe they were "pushed out" (ob129; ob317).

A teacher who has been at Mills since the first year of the consent decree observed that

> there's a lot of slack given to anybody that's considered competent, you just don't want to lose them under any circumstances. Some of the people that were kind of marginal or not willing to commit themselves, I think they got the idea, almost peer pressure, that maybe they didn't belong at Mills. They had a different philosophy of teaching. They weren't interested in working together. They didn't see education as a cooperative venture. In a couple of cases, I think the administration suggested that maybe they look some-where else, if they are not happy. It was phrased that way: "if you are not happy here." (i12.8)

Even among those faculty with closely matched beliefs and goals, dis-agreements naturally arise. While within the Brandeis faculty, conflicts tend to surface during private one-on-one conversations in hallways or class-rooms, at Mills they are more likely to emerge during open deliberation at faculty meetings. Both ephemeral and long-standing disagreements tend to be aired in the public space of meetings, though certain disputes seem to remain—as one teacher put it—"underground."

Strong community identity and permeable but discernible borders that define the community result in greater possibilities for resolving tensions. Recall, for example, that when planning for the learning challenges, one eighth-grade family had, during the previous year's planning, accused the other eighth-grade family of teachers of "stealing" their challenge idea: violence. The tension was palpable but aired during meetings—bureau-cratically sanctioned locations of influence. Though never entirely resolved, the dispute—once aired—even became common material for humor (as when Lena, one year later, stood up to say "We're just going to do what-ever 8-I is doing").

Still, differences in beliefs do exist and these can, at times, cause en-during conflict. One split, for example, concerns the extent to which par-ents should be involved in framing the curriculum. "There's no consensus on how parents should be involved in setting the agenda for the school," Elayne remarked. "It's almost a taboo topic" (i07.5). Though Mills teach-ers share a common vision of collective professional responsibility, a num-ber of teachers are uncomfortable with the faculty's tendencies to curb the influence of parents in determining curriculum. Not surprisingly, many teachers who thought that parents should be given more say in schoolwide decisions were parents themselves, in two cases, of children enrolled at Mills. One teacher who is also a parent spoke about a faculty meeting in

which a dispute arose over the policies governing the Mills Community
Council, currently a relatively marginal body that includes parents:

> One of the clear difficulties was on how much parent involvement a
> school should have. I was upset about that issue because I felt, that
> on the school level—not in my family—I felt that I was in the minor-
> ity. The faculty was coalescing against something I believe in so
> strongly. I was almost to the point of looking at another school.
> Several of us were concerned about bylaws for the Community
> Council that tried to establish a system where parents, students, and
> teachers as well as administration and other staff members, could
> come together and talk about issues and make decisions. (i08.2)

Another set of tensions revolve around what is every teacher's scarc-
est resource: time. Mills teachers participate in multiple, overlapping
teacher communities (for example, the class, the family group, subject area
department, grade-level faculty, site councils, and curriculum committees).
Once the "family" organization was instituted, some teachers felt it de-
tracted from the sense of togetherness previously engendered in connections across grades. "When we split into families, it made the school a different place," noted a teacher:

> Before we had always been looking at a schoolwide vision and
> working together as a school. Now, we were struggling to pull off
> something within a small group of teachers. . . . People were in little
> feudal territories and they couldn't really deal with other groups
> except very peripherally. The vision of a school was lost. (i12.8)

Sabrina put it this way:

> The structure we have now . . . lets people develop curriculum
> across subjects really closely, and that's one of the benefits . . . that
> lessons improve schoolwide. Yet, at the same time, it takes us away
> from that commonality. I no longer know what's going on in eighth-
> grade social studies. . . . Everything has this push and pull, you
> know, the balance dilemma. (sb57)

Some conflicts also become educational for individual teachers and,
occasionally, transformative. The Mills faculty are a thinking community,
and no one is exempt from critical analysis of their beliefs. One teacher
spoke about Jeremy's sexism and the way it manifests itself in his class.

"Jeremy's attitudes toward kids and his sense of humor that some of the kids find sexist has come up a lot. You can't observe us and not notice that it's sort of the three women against the man" (i03.30). Recall that Jeremy did not attend the summer staff development days (ob40).

> I think that he feels that we started this year angry with him because he didn't go to any of the in-service days, which pissed us off to no end because it's just incredibly unprofessional. All the catch up, all the stuff we could have talked about, could have done, and came and like told him, and he just did this real baby thing: "Oh, was there a meeting, I didn't know there was a meeting," you know refuse to say I'm sorry or anything. (i02.12)

He often does crossword puzzles during meetings. Jeremy's Awareness Month is "really awareness week" (ob42). He forgets his folder for staff development days (ob54).

And Jeremy himself recognizes his own differences in beliefs:

> Before I was just a teacher teaching Algebra, now this family stuff. In my mind I don't feel the students are learning better, there's no way to assess that, but I don't see the restructuring as being good for preparing my kids for high school. I agree the interdisciplinary stuff is a good way to learn and I like the way my family does it. . . . But math always has to accommodate other subjects; it's usually statistics or land area; they try but it's hard . . . students who are chronic absentees get hurt. (i04.1)

At times these tensions become a means for fostering growth as the teachers' beliefs evolve. Jeremy, for example, reported the following:

> I have to remember that I'm a white middle-class teacher in a consent decree school. Lena is more oriented to understanding that aspect of ethnicity and these kids' cultural backgrounds. . . . I have a hard time with lower [performing] kids, so I listen. (i04.2)

This same family of teachers, during a curriculum planning meeting about immigration, discussed the role of values and opinion in teaching. Interestingly, Jeremy, who had been only marginally engaged during most of the meeting, raised a question that resulted in a 20-minute in-depth discussion about education and the responsibility of the teacher in presenting all sides of an issue.

Difficult People or Different Beliefs?

I observed two different types of disputes that occur among the Mills faculty: those based in differences of goals, ideology, motivations, and substantive opinions; and those based in differences in commitment, understanding, and abilities. An example of the former is the familiar division found in schools between those teachers who believe parents should have considerable power to determine the content of their child's curriculum and those who believe teachers should make curricular decisions. An example of the latter is the equally common division between those teachers who devote an enormous number of hours to teaching and to the school and those who teach by the contract, arriving at school at 8:30 A.M. and departing at 3:15 P.M.; or the division between teachers who are able to present their views at meetings eloquently and with consideration to the views of others and those whose persistent soliloquies throw the meeting off track.

Reader beware: This is a matter of interpretation. One observer's notion of a brave, dissenting voice of reason in a sea of hegemonic distortions is another's notion of a troublemaker; similarly, suggesting that someone's commitment is lax can be an insidious cover for what is actually a legitimate difference in beliefs or goals (witness the patronizing invocation by members of one political constituency that members of another are less "patriotic"). I, like most case-study authors writing about school communities, am hesitant to embrace such a division and do so with great caution. And yet, the solution for so many theorists who draw on examples from the field has been to ignore these distinctions, which are so prevalent in practice. I return to this issue in Chapter 5.

MEANINGFUL RELATIONSHIPS

Early morning Friday. In a cafe across the street from the school, Eran, Raquel, and Elayne, three of the four teachers from the 6-I family, are sipping coffee. They have taken over two tables, covering them with papers outlining curricular plans for the next two months for language arts, social studies, math, and science. The teachers are focusing on developing their family's Learning Challenges, the interdisciplinary curriculum implemented schoolwide at Mills. Today's staff development day will be devoted to discussion and work around these learning challenges.

As the three teachers reach the front door of the school, papers in hand, Donna, an eighth-grade social studies teacher, is just going in. "Got it all worked out for the rest of the year?" Donna asks teasingly. They all walk into the main office, where Pasqual is playfully scolding the office secretary for telling him to come in too early for the staff development day.

"You told me it was at eight-thirty when nothing really gets started until nine," Pasqual protests.

"It's the only way we can get you here on time, Pasqual," Donna pipes up as she hands him an updated version of this year's consent decree budget, which he had asked for the previous day. As everyone in the office laughs, Lena, who has been speaking to a parent on the phone, waves her hand in the air to indicate that she cannot hear.

"I hope it's not Sharra's mother. That woman will keep her on the phone through lunch," Donna says as she looks through her mail, returning most of it to her mailbox. Lena covers the telephone handset and bites her finger in a gesture to stifle her laughter as Donna and Pasqual both head for the stairs.

"Thanks," Pasqual says as he raises the budget in the air. "I'll get the proposal to you by next week." Donna heads the budget committee this year, and Pasqual is requesting funds for a substitute teacher to help with a special schoolwide AIDS-awareness curriculum day he is planning.

These interactions foster professional relationships of a kind that go beyond the narrow requirements of designing and implementing interdisciplinary curriculum, keeping students' parents informed of their child's progress, or making school budgetary decisions. Social bonds form among teachers when they are engaged professionally in a common mission. That the sixth-grade teachers were meeting before school to plan curriculum because of their own professional commitment is certain. But equally evident was their personal and professional commitment to each other. At most meetings among faculty members, conversation moves back and forth, at times indistinguishably, from the professional to the personal.

When students from Lisa's recycling elective class come into Lena's language arts class to collect the recyclable paper, bottles, and cans, Lena gives them a message to pass on to Lisa. "Tell Ms. Clark that we're meeting today at 2:15 instead of 1:30. Also, that Elaina is picking me up after" (ob132).

Both teachers, then, during their individual classes, communicate with one another. During the class period before a sixth-grade family will attend a family-wide guest class in the library conducted by teachers from a world hunger organization, Eran's students have begun group work. His phone rings. "Yeah? What am I asking them to bring? I'm telling them to bring a piece of paper, something to write with and that summary they used last time. Does that seem right? OK, bye." A few seconds of communication breaks down the isolation between classrooms and allows teachers to check in with one another and to trade information.

During her social studies class, Donna answers the phone only to find out that a parent liaison wants a copy of the school's mission statement. "Mary, I'm in the middle of a class. Is this an emergency?" the teacher says with exasperation. When another teacher on a free period enters the room unexpectedly, Donna hands her the phone and returns to teaching. As students begin work on their current projects, the two teachers joke about pesky parent liaisons. Both end up staying to help students with their projects and then go to lunch together.

Relationships are fostered through meaningful interaction rather than through explicitly social gatherings only (though these exist as well). Teachers are not required to talk to each other in these interactions as they are during meetings. Neither is the building architecture such that teachers will inevitably cross paths. Rather, their commitment to goals they share results in high levels of interaction and communication. Teachers have a reason to talk.

The professional relationships extend to interaction with an individual teacher's involvement in other communities beyond the school walls. Lena, for example, is very involved in a creative writing group, which has yearly readings at a local studio.

> Lisa came to listen to my reading last year. I introduced her to my writing group and that meant a lot to me and I felt closer to her as a result of it. She's invited me to go hear Herman, her boyfriend, play 'cause he plays music and he's with this real wonderful group. (i01.28)

These friendships, in turn, are reflected in casual professional interactions in school. Lena continues:

> The other day [Lisa] came in here all excited and said, "You've got to come see what these kids did with this biome project. It's really wonderful." So I said OK and just dropped everything and went over there. It was the rainforest one . . . two boys worked real hard on it. And I said, "Can't I just have this in my room? It's really peaceful." And she said, "Yeah, I'm trying to wrestle it away from them." She didn't want me to come over to see what a great science teacher she was. . . . It was just "come see this." The next day, I saw

the two kids who made it in my class, and I told them, "Ms. Clark was telling me about your project. And I went over there and saw it and it's really wonderful." (i01.18)

These relationships lead to collective responsibility for the school, for students, and for each other.

CONCLUSION

Mills' teacher professional community emphasizes community ideals of participation, inclusivity, and egalitarian democracy. Strong ideological commitments bond the faculty and staff at Mills and allow for joint work toward common goals—pedagogical and beyond. Recall once again the five features of community organizing the book thus far: shared beliefs, participation, interdependence, dissent, and meaningful relationships. The Mills teachers *share beliefs* in education as a means for social change. They *participate* in many levels of community affairs. They foster *interdependent* relationships both through interdisciplinary curriculum planning and implementation and through the collective enterprise of teaching a common vision. Within a self-selected population of teachers, activities and structures encourage *dissenting opinions* to be heard. Finally, *relationships* among Mills teachers and staff merge the lives of community members outside of school (including participation in other communities) with their professional lives inside.

Mills' professional community is quite different from that of Brandeis, as described in Chapter 2. In the following two chapters, I explore both professional communities together, highlighting the ways current theoretical conceptualizations of community fail to distinguish them and the costs to practitioners, reformers, and policy analysts alike.

CHAPTER 4

Among Teacher Professional Communities

[We will] maintain a challenging learning environment . . . that fosters independence and encourages students to accept greater personal responsibility.

—Brandeis faculty

All [students] should learn to live and work in a world that is characterized by interdependence and cultural diversity.

—Mills faculty

TEACHER COMMUNITIES in schools are characterized by shared beliefs, social theorists and reformers argue. Teachers participate in community events and activities. Their work is interdependent, resulting in professional collaboration and exchange. The community allows for dissenting views and promotes tolerance and critical understanding of differing opinions. Teacher communities engender strong and multidimensional relationships among members and, as Mary Ann Raywid (1988) calls it, "an ethic of individual concern and sympathy" (p. 9). These are the characteristic features of community I detailed in Chapter 1, watchful of the ambiguity that arises when examining communities in practice.

Though both Brandeis' and Mills' teacher communities could be described by these criteria, they are, in fact, as different from one another as the epigraphs that open this chapter imply. Whereas Brandeis' professional community emphasizes teachers' individual autonomy, rights, and responsibilities to colleagues, Mills' is driven by a strong collective mission and collective values. While Brandeis' mission is broad-minded and liberal in its notion of the individual separate from the community, Mills' is specific-minded and communal in its notion of the individual in relation to the community. Brandeis' teachers seek support from one another. Mills' seek solidarity.

The dominance of current rhetoric around professional community camouflages these distinctions. In accordance with the social theory of teacher communities, both communities share beliefs, traditions, and forums in which anyone can participate. Teachers in both schools are dependent on one another for curricular and emotional support and maintain mechanisms for managing dissent. In both schools, teachers care about one another and are seen as individuals who live beyond their role as schoolteacher. Yet each of the five features of community described by social theorists take significantly different forms in these two schools. Building on the fieldwork reported thus far, the discussion below is divided into categories where these differences are especially noticeable. I then offer a stronger model for conceptualizing teacher professional community in a way that can capture these differences, emphasizing the hidden distinctions that escape the most common criteria.

DISTINGUISHING BRANDEIS' AND
MILLS' TEACHER COMMUNITIES

When I began this study, I set out to examine teacher professional communities in two well-respected middle schools. Local teachers, administrators, and scholars pointed to both Mills and Brandeis as having exemplary teacher professional communities. My plan was to describe in detail these communities, their evolution, and the processes that make them work. I knew that social theorists and school reformers use vague terms to describe communities (shared beliefs, participation, interdependence, dissent, and meaningful relationships), and I hoped to clarify them. But soon into my research I was surprised to find that not only were the terms vague in the sense of their limitations in adequately describing the communities and what they are like, but, more important, that they masked enormous differences in the goals, structures, processes, and beliefs of these communities.

I found that the features and characteristics that theorists and reformers often used to describe communities and to guide in their development tended to camouflage important differences in the schools I studied. The evidence of these differences is rendered in detail in the preceding two chapters and is summarized in Figure 4.1. Note the specific comparisons between Brandeis and Mills for each of the bulleted items within the five features of community. Under "SHARED BELIEFS," for example, Brandeis' teaching strategies are "individualized, varying depending on teacher's choice" while Mills' are "collectivized, interdisciplinary, and project based." In what follows, I discuss some of the considerable differences between the schools and their effects on the teachers, the curriculum, and the classroom.

FIGURE 4.1 Brandeis' and Mills' Different Teacher Communities

BRANDEIS	MILLS

Shared Beliefs

Purpose of schooling:

- To provide a challenging learning environment that fosters independence and personal responsibility

- To educate citizens who will (a) obey constituted authority, (b) respect the rights and property of others, and (c) maintain high personal standards of courtesy, decency, morality, honesty, and wholesome relationships

- To have each student learn at his or her maximum level

- To promote self-esteem for all students

Purpose of schooling:

- To have students learn to live and work in a world that is characterized by interdependence and cultural diversity

- To educate citizens who will (a) be informed and participating members in a democratic society, (b) lead personally fulfilling, active, and socially responsible lives, and (c) seek inclusivity, tolerance, and equity

- To critically examine local and global social issues

- To promote respect and dignity for all students

Teaching strategies:

- Individualized; vary depending on teacher's choice

- Institutional policies allow participation

Teaching strategies:

- Collectivized; interdisciplinary, project-based

- Institutional structures demand participation

Participation

- Teachers meet and discuss individual classroom teaching practices and strategies

- Teachers attend meetings and staff development days

- Administrators make decisions without input from teachers

- New teachers seek autonomy and enforce boundaries between personal and professional life

- Teachers meet and discuss shared educational principles and collective practices and strategies

- Teachers plan meetings and staff development days

- Teachers make decisions and set school policies

- New teachers drawn into climate of participation and blur personal and professional boundaries

Interdependence

- Teachers support one another's individual classroom work; occasionally team-teach (two teachers)

- Primary curricular goals are subject area defined (and therefore limited to subject area teachers)

- Teachers intertwine classroom work through collective curriculum design and implementation across subject areas

- Primary curricular goals are interdisciplinary, defined by ideals of social justice and participation

FIGURE 4.1 (continued)

BRANDEIS	MILLS
Dissent	
• Broad, generalized beliefs allow many objectives to coexist	• Openly specified beliefs result in self-selection; some teachers leave the community
• Participation in public forums is limited and selective	• Among those who remain, participation is widespread and extensive
• Dissent is rarely voiced in public forums	• Dissent is voiced in public legitimated spaces
Relationships	
• Teachers care for one another personally and professionally	• Professional and personal relationships are undistinguished
• Professional and personal (social) commitments are often in conflict	• Professional work is highly social and engages personal and social commitments

Professionalism

Brandeis is a professional community. The community is defined primarily in terms of rights and responsibilities. Teachers share ideas, have strong commitments to teaching and to children. They work hard to get along, emphasizing common ground and sometimes quashing voices of dissent. Teachers are generally content, and see themselves as blessed with hard-working and committed colleagues. Since most schools cannot boast much of a professional community, Brandeis' accomplishments are notable. In most schools, teachers feel isolated in their classrooms, and have little opportunity to come together with other teachers. At Brandeis, teachers feel generally supported, and they feel cared-for (when there is a death in the family for example, or illness). They are not "alone."

Mills is also a professional community. Teachers manage the curricular, organizational, and budgetary workings of the school. They decide on the composition of committees, sit on these committees, and make decisions that impact the school and their work. Rather than a common contracted responsibility to one another, Mills' teachers share a collective responsibility for the school and its students and a commitment to a collective mission and ideology that transcends the vicissitudes of daily practice. Dissenting voices are drawn out in legitimated spaces where they carry weight, such as meetings and planning sessions, rather than in hallways or individual classrooms where they carry less public impact.

Brandeis' professional community is a means for improving support for faculty and curriculum for students. At Mills, it is an educational aim: making communal connections, encouraging participation, and recognizing members of the school, local, and global community as interconnected comprise an educational mission for teachers and students. Brandeis' teachers come together to form what Bellah and associates called a "community of interest" (1985). For Mills' teachers, the coming together (and bringing students together in the school and in their community) is an important act in its own right.

The names the two schools use to describe their respective organizational structures offer additional clues to the differences between their conceptions of professionalism and community. Brandeis' teachers work in "teams" and Mills' work in "families." Whereas a team denotes an instrumental assemblage in which individuals come together to accomplish a task, a family indicates that individuals are part of a collective. In teams, individuals can accomplish goals together that may be unattainable alone. In families—ideally—individuals gain a sense of connection, belonging, and affinity. These differences reflect Ferdinand Tönnies' (1887/1957) oft-cited distinction between *gesellschaft* ("society" in the formal, contractual sense) and *gemeinschaft* (loosely translated as "community").

Work and Play

At Brandeis, as in most schools and perhaps most occupations, there is tension between the personal and the professional. At times, they are in conflict as when "having a life" means time for a life outside of school. Teachers share commitments to education-related aphorisms like "All children can learn" and "To grow, we must take risks" but not to any coherent ideological belief system that extends beyond their work in school. Though a number of teachers have had previous personal experiences working with other people in a way that diminished the division between work and play, at Brandeis, these teachers sought only to create meaningful ties among their students in their classrooms rather than to seek out connections with other adults in the school.

Mills, on the other hand, merges the personal and the professional into a community in which professional relationships draw in individual experiences, commitments, and stories in the service of the community. Teachers' relationships are defined less by rights and responsibilities and more by caring. Since the Mills teacher community is based on shared ideological commitments about education and about the world, their interactions are around joint work, joint ideas, and the merging of their own identities outside of work with their professional and vocational identities in work.

At Mills, the common mission blurs the lines between social, personal, and professional activities. Some teachers attend each other's writing groups, plays, and concerts. Others see each other at political rallies. Still others do not socialize with teachers outside of school, but engage in common pursuits. These activities outside of the school are extensions of their professional and ideological commitments in school. When ideologies are shared, the sense of a personal mission is fulfilled in school as well as outside. Mutual commitments to a transformative view of education promote bonds that transcend teachers' vocational (professional) and avocational (activities in addition to one's vocation) lives. Social bonds also form as a result of common world views, and therefore private and public, professional and social, are difficult to distinguish. Of course Brandeis teachers also share an ideology, but their commitments are to individual rights and responsibilities as professionals, making it more difficult to bridge disparate out-of-school commitments to joint work in school.

Another distinguishing effect between conceptions of work and play in the two professional communities can be seen in the form social celebrations take at each school. Each Brandeis faculty member embraces individual commitments and goals that may be unique to his or her classroom. The Mills faculty shares educational commitments and goals. As a result, social gatherings at Brandeis are exclusively social. They are intentional celebrations of connections to one another. Winter holiday parties, end-of-year farewell dinners, and faculty lunches are "sunshine" events (many schools have sunshine committees that plan social events for faculty). Within the Mills faculty community, on the other hand, social celebrations tend to be organized around shared goals and beliefs. Beyond social gatherings and a "time to unwind," the Mills faculty celebrate the mutual support and advancement of each other's convictions. Schoolwide faculty parties celebrating the successful implementation of a program on AIDS or "family" parties celebrating the end of the learning challenge unit on violence, for example, had organizing themes that reflected teachers' world views and educational commitments and made more fluid the connections between teachers' vocational and social lives.

Curriculum

The most obvious example of the different impact these two types of community have on the school is in the curriculum. Brandeis' sixth-grade curriculum is almost entirely individualized. To the extent that it is interdisciplinary, one teacher is teaching more than one subject rather than two or more teachers coming together. There are few joint curricular projects. Mills' curriculum is intertwined, interdependent, and interdisciplinary.

Brandeis' many curricula reflect the varied interests and commitments of individual teachers. The curriculum development process engenders sharing, storytelling, and collective reflection on individual (and occasionally team-taught) units. The collective curriculum development at Mills reflects teachers' shared beliefs about inclusivity, participation, education, and community (both the process by which they develop curriculum and the pedagogy and content of the curriculum they develop).

In the classroom, the differences are also notable. On the back wall of each Brandeis sixth-grade classroom, for example, is a chart showing the cumulative number of pages each student in the class has read this year. Each student's achievement is marked with his or her name on the chart. In the fifth week of school, in Jim's classroom, for example, an enormous cutout of a staircase shows that one student has already read 2,300 pages, one has read 1,400, while the rest are near the bottom of the chart. In a self-paced computer class, students work individually, advancing to new lessons when they have mastered current ones. On several occasions, I witnessed Brandeis teachers spend half a class period on questions about individual grades, test scoring, and relative class rankings.

At Mills, the curriculum reflects collective beliefs in the importance of community as an end in its own right, and not necessarily because students will learn more (an instrumental goal of community). In the sixth-grade family's rooftop garden project, for example, students come together in their immediate community to work on a joint project of relevance to the outside community (rather than simply for private interests). Just as teachers bridge their work within the school to their political and social commitments outside, students studied hunger in their local community (neighborhood) and related their research to issues of world hunger, or the global community. What is at play in teachers' interactions is mirrored in the curriculum they design for their students. The curriculum reflects strong beliefs in community problem solving, critical analysis, democratic participation, and inclusivity.

Classroom Management

Classroom management and discipline is a familiar middle-school headache for teachers in both schools. Teachers at Mills, however, speak about discipline problems as a collective nuisance whereas Brandeis teachers (and especially new teachers) report personal frustration and exasperation. The terminology is significant. Brandeis' and Mills' respective professional communities foster different norms around the connection between adolescent mischief and adult responsibility. When a new teacher at Brandeis has discipline problems, for example, veteran teachers come into the classroom to help, observing, making suggestions on classroom management, and occasionally using their own experience to regain and pass on classroom control.

The adult culture at Mills and its relationship to student culture makes classroom management problems into collective impediments to learning. Recall the ways Eran and Elayne handled Eran's discipline problem or the way Hannah and Pasqual handled Hannah's at Mills. Now compare these incidents with Liz's experience as a new teacher at Brandeis. Angela offered Liz technical assistance in learning to manage her own classroom while the Mills teachers made the incidents joint concerns. At Mills, private problems become public responsibilities.

Willard Waller (1932) wrote about the ways teachers rely on their colleagues for dignity: "Most of all is dignity enforced by one's fellow teachers. The significant people for a school teacher are other teachers, and by comparison with good standing in the fraternity the good opinion of students is a small thing and of little price" (p. 389). But Waller is only partially correct. Most teachers recognize early on that there is a heavy price to pay for the disapproval of students. Teachers are demoralized by discipline problems. Discipline problems at Mills are typically dealt with not by a more experienced teacher helping a new teacher (though this happens too) but rather by changing the culture of teaching entirely to one in which teachers are not primarily dependent on children for their sense of professional competence. Rather, they garner their professional respect from their colleagues while collectively addressing the classroom management needs of children.

What Waller (1932) called "dignity" is a collective enterprise at Mills. At Brandeis, teachers are supported, professionally and instrumentally, in their occasional loss of dignity ("That happens to all of us, here's how you can have better control over your classroom"), but nothing fundamental has changed about the culture of teaching, namely, that it is something you do alone. Teachers sympathize with one another and offer suggestions on how to gain better control of the classroom, but dignity continues to depend on adolescent whimsy. At Mills, teachers gain dignity from their colleagues and students and teachers alike recognize this unity. When Elayne says to her class, "I can't believe how you kids are acting out today" and then—in front of the students—to Eran: "Mr. Schwartz, I think we may have to bring the four of us together [the four family teachers] to talk about the kids' behavior and their responsibilities" the incident has become *collectively annoying* without becoming *individually humiliating* for either teacher.

A MODEL FOR DISTINGUISHING
TEACHER COMMUNITIES

Current social theories about teacher professional community do not adequately capture the differences between these communities in practice. The most commonly identified features of community, when explored empirically, leave tremendous room for variation. The result has too often been fuzzy descriptions and weak analyses and implementation strategies. In this section, I provide an exploratory model for reconceptualizing teacher professional community. By examining data from the teacher communities in the two schools that I have been calling *Louis Brandeis* and *C. Wright Mills*, I identify certain characteristics along a continuum that make it possible to distinguish these and other schools. This exploratory continuum identifies structures and processes in schools that are connected to a more complex and detailed conceptualization of a professional community. Future studies of additional schools would contribute to our understanding of the way these characteristics play out in practice in a variety of settings.

I will use the terms *liberal* and *collective* to describe two types of communities illustrated by the Brandeis and Mills faculties. A *liberal* community (and I borrow the term *liberal* from political theory) emphasizes individual rights and responsibilities. Members in a liberal community maintain individualized goals and pursue them independently. In a liberal professional community, teachers function autonomously with different goals, strategies, and practices, coming together primarily for mutual support. The guarantee of individual pursuits, argues former Supreme Court Justice Louis Brandeis, "must come mainly through a recognition of the rights of the individual" (Brandeis, 1934, p. 315). In a *collective* community, members maintain shared goals. Their tasks are intertwined and member participation in the life of the community is seen as important. In a collective community, there is a strong social contract that draws people into community life, and, as C. Wright Mills (1963) describes, promotes "the free ebb and flow of discussion" (p. 356). The work that teachers pursue in a collective professional community is interdependent and collaborative, and "virtually as many people express opinions as receive them" (p. 355).

Exploratory Continuum

Contrasting liberal teacher communities with collective teacher communities, eleven characteristics are evident along a continuum. The first eight characteristics describe features of liberal and collective teacher communities (see Figure 4.2). Below, I use the now familiar portraits of the

FIGURE 4.2 Characteristic Features of Teacher Communities

LIBERAL		COLLECTIVE
Community relations are increasingly defined by rights and responsibilities	1	Community relations are increasingly defined by caring and interdependence
Individual work and responsibility for students, curriculum, and discipline	2	Joint work and responsibility for students, curriculum, and discipline
Teacher discourse is limited to students, problems, and curriculum ideas and strategies	3	Teacher discourse includes purposes, principles, and philosophies of education
School management is hierarchical with leadership through ascribed title	4	School management is diffuse with leadership through talent recognition
Private (classroom) problems elicit advice and sympathy	5	Private problems are public responsibilities
Few voices are heard in public forms; dissent is submerged and, when expressed, marginalized	6	Many voices are heard in public forums; dissent is drawn out and transforms the community, is transformed to better match the community, is tolerated, or is cause for leaving the community
Sense of instrumental worth of the community	7	Sense of intrinsic worth of the community
Sense of anonymity, homogeneity, and conformity within the community	8	Sense of individuality and identity within the community

Brandeis and Mills faculty to show what distinguishes these eight characteristic features of liberal and collective communities in practice.

1. Professional relationships in liberal teacher communities like Brandeis'
   emphasize rights and responsibilities to colleagues. Most Brandeis teachers collaborate with their team partners because of a liberal commitment
   to support one another in individual practice. Relationships in collective communities like Mills—with its shared commitment to ideals of
   participation and community—are characterized by affinity, solidarity,
   and caring. Most Mills teachers work together out of collective commitments to common values and a community-oriented spirit.
2. Brandeis' professional community emphasizes personal responsibility
   both among teachers and in the curriculum for students. "There's room
   to disagree and there's room to do it differently" (i01.16). Individual
   responsibility for individual students rather than collective responsibility for the student community is the norm in Brandeis' liberal teacher
   community. Joint work is emphasized at Brandeis only to the extent that
   it facilitates individual teachers in achieving individual goals. The collective professional community at Mills is characterized by joint responsibility for many aspects of teaching. Teachers emphasize joint work and
   collective projects not only because joint work can accomplish some tasks
   that solitary work cannot, but also because joint work is a community
   ideal that engenders participation, interaction, and interdependent
   relationships.
3. Discussion among Brandeis teachers centers around issues of practice
   and pedagogy. Teachers share ideas and stories about their teaching and
   about students. Since the educational principles that guide Brandeis
   teachers vary substantially, public conversation and exchange focuses
   on noncontroversial adaptations of curricular ideas and strategies rather
   than on purposes and principles, or philosophies of education. Discussion among teachers at Mills is frequently filled with exchanges that
   explore principles and philosophies of education. While McLaughlin
   and Talbert's recent work on teacher communities (McLaughlin, 1993;
   Talbert, 1993) suggests that discourse about principles represents an evolutionary stage of community (which can arise after stages of teacher
   talk about students, problems, and strategies), my findings suggest otherwise. Mills teachers engaged in discourse on educational purposes and
   principles from their first day together when the first principal after
   reconstitution asked new teachers to write down what was important
   to them for a school. Philosophical discussions about education take
   place at many faculty, family, and department meetings as well as in

informal conversation. Whereas both communities were three years old at the time of this study, Mills teachers talked frequently about the purpose of schooling and educational principles that guide them, while Brandeis teachers did so much less.

4. At Brandeis, school management positions are appointed and are hierarchical. Recall that the principal assigns teachers to the two sixth-grade instructional supervisor positions and that these ascribed titles translate, as intended, to supervisory control over most budgetary and management decisions. At Mills, stronger relationships of affinity and greater number of opportunities for teachers to know each other's strengths result in hierarchies defined more by abilities and less by ascribed titles. Through ample collective work, individuals are known for their talents rather than their positions. More frequent participation and recognition of individual contributions to the community allow for a greater knowledge of individual talents and abilities.

5. Private problems among Brandeis teachers result in advice-seeking. Individual teachers offer sympathy and guidance to other individual teachers in need—a cornerstone of liberal commitments. At Mills, private problems are public and collective responsibilities. If a Mills teacher is having a discipline problem with students, for example, the "family" of teachers takes up the issue collectively.

6. Brandeis teachers talk relatively little in public forums. Disagreements, especially, are voiced much less often in public contexts such as meetings or staff development days. Brandeis teachers are likely to voice dissenting opinions in private: informal conversations in classrooms or hallways. Mills teachers participate in all levels of community decision making and planning. Dissenting opinions are frequently voiced. Schools such as Mills are more likely to foster participation and less likely to result in the marginalization or silencing of dissenting views. Individuals with dissenting opinions at Mills either transform the community, are transformed to better match the community, are tolerated, or depart from the community. No teachers have left Brandeis over disagreements in principles or values. It is easier for Brandeis teachers to maintain disparate beliefs since work is more autonomous. Mills demonstrates greater exclusivity in member selection.

7. Whereas individuals in a liberal teacher community have an instrumental understanding of community commitments, teachers in a collective community emphasize—at times instinctively—the intrinsic importance of communal attachments and bonds. While Brandeis teachers see community as a means, Mills teachers see it as an end. The Mills teacher community is characterized by a sense of intrinsic worth. The focus on

the intrinsic rather than the instrumental value of community places schools like Mills at odds with current policy and reform rhetoric. I revisit this distinction in Chapter 5.

8. At Brandeis, conformity to norms of professionalism and individual autonomy provides few opportunities for individuals to establish a unique identity through participation in community affairs. Individual expression is less likely to emerge within the teacher community at Brandeis than at Mills. Contrary to the common fear of loss of individuality within community, Mills teachers gain a sense of individual identity specifically through their participation in community affairs. I elaborate on the compatability of individuality and community in detail in Chapter 5.

Like these 8 features of communities, numbers 9 through 11 also characterize the differences between liberal and collective teacher professional communities. These next three features of community, however, not only describe what the community looks like, but, at the same time, how it got to be that way. They are both *features of* and *processes to* community. I will call these "contributing features" to emphasize that they both describe the community and give clues to its formation (see Figure 4.3).

FIGURE 4.3 Contributing Features and Processes

LIBERAL		COLLECTIVE
Loose hiring criteria based on broad commitments to children and to teaching	9	Selective hiring criteria based on shared beliefs about collaboration, participation, and joint work
Perfunctory faculty activities allow but do not require participation	10	Structured faculty activites ensure participation and promote a climate of participation
Curricular goals emphasize personal initiative and individual rights and responsibilities for both teachers and students	11	Curricular goals emphasize interdependence and collective action among both teachers and students

9. Brandeis teachers are hired under loose criteria based on broad educational commitments. Though the criteria could be considered selective (almost all the teachers came from within the Bayland district), it had little to do with teachers' philosophy of teaching or any shared outlook or convictions. Mills is characterized by a selective hiring process. Mills teachers either were screened for beliefs about collaboration, participation, and joint work by the hiring committee ("I was really strongly committed to the idea of working as a team" [i05.9]) or they self-screened ("I had my fingers in the pie with a lot of schools [but] I decided to go here because of the entrenched collective atmosphere" [i05.1–3]).

   A selective process of hiring that might be employed by schools seeking to become collective communities like Mills also has implications for the forms of administration and leadership it makes possible. Studies of leadership have found that leaders successful in bringing groups together around a common mission often begin with a clear vision and purpose at the same time that they encourage participation (Immegart, 1988). It is notable that, at Brandeis, the principal arranged for the superintendent to come to the first faculty meeting to "deliver" a vision for the new sixth grade. Such a top-down approach to vision-setting provides a clear vision at the expense of participation. At Mills, on the other hand, the founding principal of the reconstituted Mills provided new teachers with a blank piece of paper on which they constructed their vision. At first glance, one might conclude that no vision was provided by the administration. In reality, the Mills principal had a clear enough vision to hire faculty who, when presented with a blank piece of paper, would agree on certain basic premises of his vision whereas Brandeis' hiring process did not tend to screen for a particular educational vision. Moreover, when the Mills faculty's vision later strayed from the one the principal had in mind, he stepped in to guide it, having already gained their trust.

10. The Brandeis faculty community is marked by perfunctory activities and structures, which allow but do not require participation. In a liberal community, participation is allowed but not required. The Mills faculty community sustains institutional structures, activities, and traditions that explicitly promote a climate of participation. Balancing tradition and structure with innovation and latitude, the Mills teacher community succeeds in breaking expectations of autonomy and solitary work (Little, 1990), providing instead a professional culture characterized by participation and mutual engagement.

11. Brandeis' educational mission and curricular goals for students reflect the faculty's focus on personal initiative and individual rights and re-

sponsibilities for teachers. Conversely, the Mills faculty commitment to collaborative work is reflected in the emphasis on collaboration in the student curriculum. Curriculum at Mills is characterized by explicit emphasis on building a schoolwide collective community that underscores interdependent relationships, collective action and reflection, and belonging (for both teachers and students).

Points on the Continuum

A professional community oriented around liberal individualist priorities is clearly quite different from one organized around collective goals. Each represents distinct working cultures for faculty and staff and results in distinctive educational climates for students. In this chapter, I have specified these differences and constructed a provisional model to capture the structures, processes, and characteristics associated with liberal and collective manifestations of teacher professional communities.

Brandeis and Mills would fall on different points along the continuum for each characteristic. They would not necessarily be polar opposites in all cases. Brandeis is not a community purely defined by liberal individualist tendencies across all the features of a liberal community; nor is Mills purely collective. These binary end points are not either/or but rather constitute the playing field of conceptual space on which the teachers in each school make their organizational and interpersonal decisions. While it is hard to imagine teachers in a school that resembles current school organization to be engaged in any more joint work than Mills' teachers (see feature 2 in Figure 4.2), for example, one does not have to look far for a school in which teachers are more isolated in their work than at Brandeis. The Mills teacher community falls on the collective side of the "joint work" continuum. Brandeis' teacher community falls somewhere in between Mills and the traditional one-room schoolhouse or a comprehensive high school in which teachers teach their own subject in their own classroom five periods per day with little collegial contact.

Similarly, Brandeis' teacher relationships, though not indicative of a collective ideological "solidarity" oriented around the joint pursuit of a common vision for society, do manifest caring. In theoretical discourse, liberal communities defined by rights and responsibilities are typically characterized by purely instrumental relationships. When the need for community is no longer evident (the goal has been achieved or made obsolete), the relationships disintegrate. Brandeis' teachers, however, unquestionably care for one another beyond narrow instrumental ends. Again, Brandeis' teacher community falls somewhere between the end points of the continuum.

Though Mills' hiring practices resulted in a certain degree of selectivity, one could imagine forming a school staff based on a much more overt screening process. The elements of this continuum do not all use Brandeis and Mills as their end points. Rather, the characteristics of teacher professional community that each highlights represent a broad range and a conceptual framework that might be applied to an exploration of other schools and other teacher communities.

By forcing the distinction between liberal and collective communities, and by looking specifically at the Brandeis and Mills professional communities, however, researchers, reformers, and policymakers can draw valuable lessons for studying, describing, and fostering teacher professional communities at other sites and understanding the tensions and complexities inherent in such work. These lessons are the subject of the following chapter.

CHAPTER 5

Two Cases, Three Lessons

Our form of government, as well as humanity, compels us to
strive for the development of the individual man.
                                    —Louis D. Brandeis (1914/1933, p. 366)

Today, the personal and the social ideals of knowledge have
coincided. . . . Only when knowledge has public relevance is
[democracy] possible.
                                    —C. Wright Mills (1963, p. 19)

IN THE RENEWED emphasis on educational reform that has characterized the last decade, teachers' professional relationships have been
the target of many school reorganization efforts (Barth, 1990; Lieberman, 1988b, 1990; Rosenholtz, 1989). Teacher professional communities are
seen as a promising solution to a profession wrought with isolation. But,
while inroads have been made under the rubric of teacher professionalization, many reform efforts aimed at fostering teacher community have
met with resistance. Others have vanished amidst the intractability of traditional school culture and organization.

Maxine Greene speaks of a "new camaraderie" needed among teachers (1986) and calls for teacher participation in fostering democratic communities for themselves and their students (1985). Milbrey McLaughlin and
Sylvia Yee (1988) echo the findings of numerous researchers that successful schools "are differentiated from less successful ones by the norms of
interaction" (p. 35). And the Bush administration's "America 2000: An Education Strategy" called for more teacher involvement in decision making
and professed support for the professional, more autonomous teacher
(Department of Education, 1991). There are dozens of others: supporters
in academia, in practice, and in government all of whom call for some vision of teacher collegiality, professional collaboration, and professional
autonomy (see, for example, Eisner, 1984; Meier, 1985; Sergiovanni, 1989;
Shanker, 1987; Zeichner, 1991).

I do not group this diverse list of community advocates in an effort to gloss over their significant differences in perspective. Let me state clearly that Maxine Greene's understanding of the forces at work on schools and their personnel have little in common with that of Lamar Alexander, Secretary of Education in the Bush administration. It is notable, however, that calls for transforming the workplace of teachers to make it more professional, more collegial, and more communal come from a very disparate group of reformers. Few argue against enhancing teacher communities in schools.

Why, then, does the task of achieving the type of collegial setting that so many calls for reform suggest seem so elusive? Because there are no agreed-on models: These reformers are talking about very different types of professional community.

Brandeis' liberal professional community and Mills' collective one differ in the beliefs teachers share, the ways they interact and participate in the life of the community, the degree to which the curriculum and management of the school make them interdependent, and the ways they negotiate dissent and relationships within the community. Critics of community have downplayed these differences. They have failed to emphasize adequately the ways in which successful communities rely on particular belief systems and ideologies and require a carefully balanced combination of structures and processes, traditions and space for innovations. One can value dissent, but without creating the institutional structures, processes, and policies that demand it, it is unlikely to be vocalized. In fact, some studies of participation in democratic processes such as debate and voting suggest that dissenting opinions, when not vocalized, may actually cease to exist. Because of a dearth of structured opportunities for participation, in other words, teachers' thinking would increasingly reflect dominant communitywide and homogenous ideas, thereby suppressing not only the expression of dissent but also its formulation (see, for example, Paulo Friere's *Pedagogy of the Oppressed*, 1970). Moreover, the value system, common goals, and shared beliefs that give the community a clear sense of mission, a collective identity, and an ideology are too often obscured in policy rhetoric.

CLARIFYING REFORM GOALS
FOR TEACHER COMMUNITIES

How is teacher professional community built, sustained, and advanced? From this study of two California middle schools, one urban and the other suburban, we learn three important lessons. To the degree that teachers, administrators, researchers, and policymakers seek to clarify the beliefs and goals represented by their efforts, these lessons would apply. Moreover, social theorists and reformers interested in broader conceptions of community and democracy will find embedded in these lessons both the clarity and complexity gleaned from in-depth study and analysis of particular communities in practice.

Lesson 1: Beliefs Matter

That members of communities share beliefs seems to be somewhat of a truism in current philosophical debates. Of the various characteristics and features of community that I detailed in Chapter 1, "shared beliefs" is by far the condition of community most often mentioned.[1] Accordingly, in a growing body of school reform literature, shared beliefs play a prominent role in the various recipes, guidelines, and discussions that surround efforts to build teacher professional communities in schools. Surprisingly, however, there is little discussion of the nature of the beliefs. "What beliefs should be shared?" is a thorny question almost always left to the imagination of practitioners and policymakers.

In *Building Community in Schools* (1994), for example, Thomas Sergiovanni argues that schools need a common vision. They need focus and clarity about their beliefs and values. But he goes on to argue that

> the subject matter of this focus and clarity may well be secondary. . . . When accounting for the success of certain schools—"back to basics" Christian fundamentalist schools, Coalition of Essential Schools, Catholic parish schools, magnet public schools, ungraded elementary schools, or just plain-vanilla schools—the specifics of their undergirding educational philosophy may not be key. Philosophies among successful schools differ, often dramatically. Instead, success seems to be related to the fact that though substance differs, the schools have achieved focus and clarity and have embodied them in a unified practice. (p. 100)

To illustrate, he presents the reader with various "successful" schools' mission statements. "Is what we're doing consistent with what we believe?" becomes the guiding question schools should ask in order to become authentic communities (p. 109). He is not alone in this emphasis. Many other reformers and theorists agree that the coherence, strength, and history of

---

1. There are exceptions, but they are few. Joseph Maxwell (1994), for example, argues that what is important is not shared beliefs but "contiguity" or continuous and reliable interaction and participation.

shared beliefs contribute to the vitality and stability of the community (Newmann & Oliver, 1967; Raywid, 1993; Louis, Marks, & Kruse, 1994; Louis & Kruse, 1995; Scherer, 1972; Selznick, 1992). They assert the role that *sharing beliefs* plays in community-building while ignoring the importance of the nature of the beliefs themselves.

Many schools that advocate strong teacher professional communities boast mutual shared obligations and commitments. But these are often slogans such as "acceptance of all children" or "a desire to serve ideals." Whose ideals? What do these teachers believe in? What kind of world do they strive for? Avoiding these more difficult and complex concerns, many researchers and reformers maintain that what is important is that beliefs are shared. But do they care whether the beliefs that are shared are worth sharing?

Clearly they do. Examples of shared beliefs cited in case studies of "successful schools" are ones on which most advocates of building community in schools can agree: Members always believe in participation, inclusivity, and strong relationships. Even the Christian fundamentalist school in Sergiovanni's (1994) book—usually representing the type of educational philosophy invoked to demonstrate the difficulties of wholeheartedly embracing notions of community—has a special emphasis on multicultural curriculum and hopes to help students "go beyond sympathy to empathy when viewing other cultures" (p. 101).

But what about the more controversial fundamentalist schools like the one portrayed in Alan Peshkin's *God's Choice* (1986)? Alasdair MacIntyre (1981) and Allan Bloom (1987) would both prefer a return to traditional communities with "traditional" values. Schools based on these beliefs would look different from those based on John Dewey's (1916) vision of a democratic school.

Sergiovanni (1994) and others who describe communities in practice portray agreeable schools. By using ideologically palatable examples of beliefs that faculties share and maintaining all the while that the content of the beliefs is not important, Sergiovanni evades the obligation of exploring which beliefs succeed and which fail to engender communities that manage conflict and ensure full participation of members with a diversity of backgrounds and interests. We can all agree that schools must have a common purpose. But the purpose matters, not just the act of having one, and here is where Sergiovanni's guidelines end and the truly difficult work of community-building begins. Sergiovanni writes:

> Schools can become [among other types of community] inclusive communities where differences are brought together into a mutually respectful whole [but] schools must first become places where members have developed a

community of mind that bonds them together in a special way and binds them to a shared ideology. (p. xvii)

In the everyday life of schools, the beliefs and the ideology, as well as how they are elicited, count. There are philosophical, political, and ideological commitments that allow people to make relationships priorities, to create spaces that are inclusive and a school culture that is community-oriented. These commitments are sometimes incompatible with, for example, a belief that the major books of one culture represented in the school community are less important for the curriculum than those of another or support of a law that denies one group of children of the community education or health services.

The 11 characteristics of teacher community described in Chapter 4 illustrate these differences along a liberal-collective continuum. While Brandeis teachers are hard working and deeply committed to teaching, they are committed to the individual development of their students and their classroom autonomy as professionals. They are not committed to a collective pedagogy or community-building processes. As a result, opportunities for continuing participation and interaction occur far less at Brandeis than at Mills and, when they do, are instrumentally aimed at enhancing individualism. Participation is diminished at Brandeis and tensions are hidden. Mills' beliefs, on the other hand, are ideologically predisposed to collective work, to inclusion, to change, and to an emphasis on interdependent relationships.

Similarly, while Brandeis teachers share beliefs in the importance of collaboration for student learning and professional growth, Mills teachers share beliefs in the importance of community as an end. Brandeis' teacher community serves instrumental purposes. Mills' serves intrinsic commitments. Policy rhetoric has had a distinctly instrumental flavor, making Brandeis more consistent with many current reformers' visions of the purposes and practices of teacher professional community: Stronger teacher communities will reduce absenteeism and increase professionalism; stronger school communities will raise student test scores and reduce student dropout rates. Barth (1990), Sarason (1971), and McLaughlin (1992a, 1992b) all point to the need to connect teacher community to student learning. Reformers have failed to confront whether community is outcome-oriented or a significant goal in its own right and what it would mean not to sidestep the latter.

"The structure can be seen as helping kids," one Brandeis teacher explained, "or it can be seen as just helping teachers, for the convenience" (i12.17). In comparison, a new Mills teacher observed:

> I think the families do tremendous good for the kids, but the first year I couldn't even focus on that. I was only focusing on how the family related to me, and I found it very supportive. The second and third year I was able to think about what a great structure the families were for kids. (ob12)

The beliefs that Mills teachers share engender community ideals. They are fundamentally different from shared beliefs that work at cross purposes to building community.

A further example: The Brandeis curriculum emphasizes individual rights and ability tracking to the exclusion of certain members of the community. Ability tracking at Mills is seen as conflicting with community norms of inclusivity. At one Mills faculty meeting, for example, Tom Connor, the principal, was explaining a possible process for nominating students for participation in before-school classes for the upcoming Educational Testing Service's PSAT exams. Lena asked how students would be nominated for the PSAT list. When Tom responded that students would be eligible through voluntary recommendations from teachers or parents, Pasqual nominated the entire list of students on "detention" that week: "I'd like to recommend the Tuesday/Thursday detention class for PSATs Mr. Connor" (ob269). A round of critique of tracking followed including comments such as "These opportunities should be available to all of our students" and "This kind of ability grouping is divisive for the student body" (ob270).

Brandeis is characterized by an announcement I heard over the school's public address system. A student, broadcasting to all the classrooms, made a series of announcements. After an apology for the late-afternoon interruption, the student closed with "And now the thought for the day: Do unto others as you would have others do unto you. Keep smiling" (ob76). The notion of the individual at Mills, on the other hand, is community-defined. Rather than the individual in isolation, individuals are defined in their relationships with others. Most Mills teachers maintain the importance of connection, consistent with community theorists and even theologians such as Martin Buber or Paul Tillich: "Only in the continuous encounter with other persons does the person become and remain a person. The place of this encounter is the community" (Tillich, 1952, p. 91).

C. Wright Mills (1963) highlights some of these differences in distinguishing between what he calls a *public* and a *mass*:

> In a *public* as I understand the term, virtually as many people express opinions as receive them; public communications are so organized that there is a

chance immediately and effectively to answer back to any opinion expressed in public. . . . When these conditions prevail, we have [a model that] fits pretty closely the several assumptions of classic democratic theory. (p. 355)

In a *mass*, conversely, "far fewer people express opinions than receive them; for the community . . . becomes an abstracted collectivity of individuals" (p. 355). In both C. Wright Mills—the person's—conception of the *public* and C. Wright Mills—the school's—conception of collective work lies a common understanding of the strength and possibilities that can come from connection and affiliation. Power, Hannah Arendt (1972) wrote, is the ability of people "to get together and act in concert" (p. 151). Shared beliefs in the power of getting together and acting in concert, in participation, and in ensuring that marginalized voices are heard are important not only for the fact that they are shared, but also that they reflect ideals of participatory and egalitarian communities. The content of the beliefs matter.

Lesson 2: Structures Matter

The educator is responsible for a knowledge of individuals and for a knowledge of subject-matter that will enable activities to be selected which lend themselves to social organization, an organization in which all individuals have an opportunity to contribute something, and in which the activities in which all participate are the chief carriers of control. (Dewey, 1938, p. 56)

John Dewey directed his comments to teachers, whose responsibilities, he argued, included carefully selecting activities that encourage social bonds and communal organization. The same can be said for those teachers and administrators selecting activities (and designing structures) for teachers. Recall the differences, illustrated by the liberal-collective continuum, between structures for participation at Brandeis and those at Mills. In Chapter 3 on Mills, I used the term *planned inclusivity* to indicate the presence of structures that prod teachers to take part in the professional life of the community. In this section I focus on structures that ensure participation by all members of the community and structures that manage dissent.

The Mills faculty strikes a careful balance between institutionalized structures and enduring innovation. Educators—and ironically progressive educators who value communities in particular—worry about imposed structures. They assume that enduring structures are authoritarian or condescending and pit them against notions of professionalism and commitment to a democratic workplace. Jonathan Kozol's (1972) *Free Schools*, for example, portrays schools in which teachers' commitments to egalitarian organization without hierarchies often led to reconstruction of traditional power inequities or to chaos.[2] Yet very specific structures were essential at various stages of evolution of the Mills teacher community. In the opening meeting of the year, for example, teachers were more or less compelled to participate (in this example, in a small way) by reporting something about their summer activities, creating an environment in which even new teachers were drawn into a temporary and somewhat artificial but firmly structured culture of participation. After the structure was in place (here initiated by the principal), the "introductions no longer require[d] Mr. Conner to emcee" and the culture of participation endured in a more natural way. The short life of the (artificial) structure had served its purpose.

There are far fewer explicit structures in place at Brandeis to foster participation and manage conflict. Those that are in place—because they don't revolve around more significant shared beliefs—tend to stay as artificial games and never transmute into deeper forms of interaction and participation as they do at Mills (where they also began as artificial or "forced" games). Forms for participation are present (facilitator, recorder, etc.) at Brandeis, but they are embraced as useful organizational mechanisms and not as structures to enhance participation and interdependence, and honor dissent. The rotating facilitator at Brandeis, for example, does not prepare for meetings, but simply reads off the agenda and serves as timekeeper. In fact, the facilitator is often decided on minutes before the meeting.

On the other hand, there are structures in place at Mills for collective planning, for talking at meetings and staff development days, for assigning responsibilities, and for contributing to the community in accordance with one's talents and abilities. Lena, for example, spoke about skits that the faculty write, direct, and perform together:

> I think planning and performing these skits was really a way where we gave voice to everybody that was involved and it wasn't like whoever had the loudest mouth or something. It was a way of asking "what's bothering you with your kids, what would you like to see us include in here?" There was a way that everything was very inclusive. So when these things would go off on the stage, everybody had a little buying into it. And if we flopped, we flopped together and if we were good, we could all feel good together. And I think that that feeling is somewhat alive. . . . It makes teaching in that kind of environment so energizing, so alive. (i01.79)

---

2. Interestingly, this echoes the debate within the Progressive Education Association around child-centered education that eventually led John Dewey to disavow his connection with the association. For a discussion of this debate, see Graham (1967).

Mills' structures encourage involvement—sometimes artificially—to counteract the dominant notion that participation is somehow compromising and that individual autonomy is at odds with participation.

Where Brandeis tends toward the model of democracy that is more like the one at work in the larger society—everyone can vote, but fewer than half do, Mills relies heavily on the use of teachers' stories, drawn out in explicit structured activities that require participation by everyone, including the weak, the marginal, and the different.

In *Distinction* (1984), Pierre Bourdieu discusses the self-elimination of voice that is so common in contemporary democracies and is mirrored in the Brandeis teacher professional community. Bourdieu points out that large percentages of people surveyed abstain from answering questions on politics (answering "I don't know," for example). "What needs to be questioned," he argues, "is the very notion of 'personal opinion' . . . [since it] credits everyone not only with the right but also the power to produce such a judgement" (p. 398).

Bourdieu's study of why certain people vote and others don't helps explain the fact that at Brandeis—and many other schools—only a few teachers ever talk at faculty meetings. Self-elimination of voice may well come from a lack of structure and results in what Bourdieu calls "selective democracy":

> The indulgent populism [in the case of community discourse, the dominance of rhetoric of inclusivity] which credits the common people with innate knowledge of politics equally helps to disguise and so consecrate the "concentration in a few individuals" of the capacity to produce discourse about the social world [i.e., opinions actually being voiced] and, through this, the capacity for consciously changing that world. (1984, p. 397)

This is not to say that Brandeis offers less of an education than Mills. It does not. Students seem engaged and teachers generally like teaching there. Marginal students and—more important for this book—marginal teachers, however, are more marginalized. Their particular talents are less utilized, they interact in collective projects less. And they do not voice their thoughts in public or "above ground" places where they have impact, preferring underground places where they do not.

> Even if one only credits the idealized "people" with a wholly practical knowledge of the social world as such, or at least its position and interests in the world, one still has to examine whether, and how, this political sense can be expressed in a discourse corresponding to the truth it contains in practical form, and thus become the motor of a conscious and, through the mobilizing power of explicit statement, truly collective action. (Bourdieu, 1984, p. 398)

At Mills, most decisive actions are collective. At Brandeis, while decisions are not authoritarian, they are also not collectively made, mostly because people opt out of their stake in the community. Some teachers felt that they were not competent to make the decisions:

> This capacity is inseparable from a more or less strong feeling of being *competent*, in the full sense of the word, that is, socially recognized as entitled to deal with political affairs, to express an opinion about them or even modify their course. (Bourdieu, 1984, p. 399, emphasis in original)

Others felt simply that they were not being asked to participate and therefore would rather not. In either case, the result is nonparticipation in sixth-grade team and schoolwide decisions. Bourdieu's argument about participation in national politics, then, may apply to these local settings. Electoral democracy that grants everyone the right and duty to have an opinion and technocratic aristocracy, which restricts opinion to "experts" elected for "intelligence" and "competence," are not all that different since in electoral democracy citizens "self-exclude."

The implications of this study inform the larger philosophical discourse on democracy. Bourdieu (1984) does not suggest an antidote to the problem of selective democracy. While this study does not speak directly to democracy in civic life, in the relatively small arena of site-based managed schools, the findings suggest variations in the meaning of community participation and the relation of particular structures to real, and not simply condoned, participation.

These structures show differences in the two teacher communities studied and reflect differences in the beliefs about community that I presented in Lesson 1. Mills' teacher community indicates that structure does not necessarily take away from freedom; in fact, in this community, structures engender freedom. They are provisional structures that incorporate in their definition the possibility of their change. They are based on the premise that every voice *is* heard and not that every voice can be heard.

Similarly, contrary to current debates that dichotomize individuality and community, community does not necessarily take away from individuality. It may actually foster it. I explore this next point in Lesson 3.

Lesson 3: Individuality and Community Are Unexpected Bedfellows

Brandeis' sixth-grade teachers comprise what theorists call a liberal community, characterized by individual freedoms, rights, and responsibilities. In such communities, there exists a common tension and fear: that within a community with shared beliefs and interests, individuality will be suppressed and the individual submerged into a monolithic whole. Though Brandeis is not an example of a community in which individual rights and freedoms are protected at all costs to the exclusion of any communal attachments, it does offer a sufficient contrast to Mills' teacher community. Teachers at Brandeis know each other as individuals; however, the knowledge is limited to what teachers can gain through only a modest degree of collective participation. Angela knows that Valerie goes to a cabin during the summer with her husband but not that Mike paints. Jim knows that Leslie was sick for two weeks, but not that she listens to music when she works.

Among the teachers, administrators, and staff at Mills are the usual gamut of individuals as well: the gregarious and the reserved, the associated and the isolated, those who stand out and those who prefer to blend in. Teachers are well known for their talents, their abilities, and their idiosyncracies. Marty was "a real ham," Lena notes when describing the skits they used to perform. Others are known for writing the music, painting the set, or simply typing and photocopying the scripts. Each is recognized for his or her contribution. This kind of interaction and participation lends itself specifically to individuals' gaining an identity within the community. "She's the funny one." "He's so articulate." "She has a real calming affect on people."

Even negative attributes become part of individual identities within the group that diminish each person's sense of anonymity. "Pasqual's at it again! Someone turn him off for two minutes." "I'm not surprised Lloyd asked about that. He's incredibly meddlesome and annoying." These are often said with more affection than contempt.

Individual teachers in the faculty community at Mills gain (rather than lose) a sense of identity and individuality through their participation in the community. This calls into question critics' customary polarization of the individual and the collective. The opening meeting, in this case, serves only as evidence of processes that took place before. At this meeting, I learned an extraordinary amount about individuals' multiple roles in the community, their hopes, their skills, and their idiosyncracies—their identities *in relation to* the community. Before Walter, the music teacher, had opened his mouth to speak, for example, someone from across the room yelled that he should speak louder. The entire faculty erupted in laughter. Walter smiled too and then began the tale of his cross-country train trek. Walter is known for speaking quietly. Paul builds wheelchairs. Mark is a workhorse. Sabrina is active in local community politics and can be counted on to bring important aspects of her work to bear in curriculum development for the school. Eran won a Fulbright. Lena enjoys and is good at planning staff development. Tom just married his third wife. Through interaction and participation within the community, identities emerge, and individuality (as difference) is embraced rather than suppressed.

In a culture of participation, many teachers and other staff members have pet projects for which they are known. Consequently, identity and status within the community rely more on these types of recognized contributions than on titular or bureaucratically sanctioned roles (see Kruse, Louis, & Bryk, 1995). Consider, for example, Pato, a teacher's aide at Mills who happens also to be a photographer. For several months, Pato's photographs shot at various events during the school year were displayed in the school lobby, beautifully printed, matted, and framed. The show was called "Untitled Moments from the Mills Series" and was accompanied by the following explanation:

> I am interested in the presence of art in everyday places. . . . Being young and working as a paraprofessional, I sometimes feel that I'm working in the spaces between students, teachers, administrators, counselors, and other "classified personnel." I often spend my lunch hour on the playground with the students. The playground is one of few places in school where students are more or less in charge of what happens. I am interested in the mixing of people in this space. . . . I distribute wallet-size pictures to all students who want them. This helps to give me a more immediate connection to the people I photograph . . . it also helps me to develop relationships which aren't totally defined by me being an "adult" and them being "children." . . . By making and sharing my work here, I am not some strange unknown "artist" but a creative person doing his everyday work.

Paraprofessionals are often marginal to school communities. Here Pato has an identity as an artist/photographer within the school and is recognized for his art. Moreover, the very foundation of his art is created in interaction with the members of the school community. They become part of his art. Within the Mills community, Pato's identity as an artist is inseparable from his identity as a participant ("I am not some strange unknown artist"). Conversely, his identity as a teacher's aide is inseparable from his art.

Smaller, transient forms of participation and identity-making may be equally important. One afternoon, Lena needed a drawing for a lesson she was preparing and asked Sabrina, who draws well, to help her (ob194). On another afternoon, Eran walked down the back stairwell singing because the echo made his voice reverberate grandiosely. Ben, the school custodian, joined in with the same pitch, behind his cart, mop in hand (ob281).

"I don't feel like there's a set hierarchy," remarked a teacher new to Mills. "I feel like there's a sense of what people do best. That Eran maybe understands scheduling better than other people. Or Elayne is better at assessment. And Raquel's good at keeping an agenda going" (i08.2).[3]

Individual identities are especially apparent when teachers engage in collective projects such as the skits or developing the learning challenges. These collective projects do not downplay individual differences. At their best, they showcase teachers' talents and model the use of these talents for social purposes. Talents and identities, however, are obvious in virtually all formal and informal encounters from faculty meetings to lunchtime conversation. Rather than submerging the individual within the group, collective work and frequent and engaged participation provide an opportunity and forum to develop an individual identity within and in relation to the group.

THE IMPORTANCE OF STRONGER MODELS
FOR TEACHER COMMUNITY

Why should we care about conceptualizing community and examining communities in practice? Why, for example, do beliefs and structures matter? Because without richer and more careful conceptualizations and explorations, school reform efforts end up rudderless and the rhetoric of "community" is rendered ubiquitous and shallow. Community, as we have seen in the preceding chapters, is not a universally defined outcome. It is a way of travelling with a new view. Certainly and rigorously debating what that view should be is the task researchers, practitioners, and policymakers now face.

Future Directions for Researchers

Researchers could benefit from a stronger conceptualization of communities based in empirical research. The lessons learned from two California middle schools as well as the continuum in the previous chapter strengthen current conceptualizations of community that have remained vague and estranged from the complexities of professional communities

---

3. Bureaucratically, of course, there is a hierarchy. Both the principal and vice principal have higher salaries than teachers, who in turn have higher salaries than Pato, the paraprofessional. Site-based management, as a reform strategy, seeks to give teachers greater control over their work environment, but does not address status differentials between teachers and administrators.

in practice. This study examines teacher communities in only two schools. As more case studies explore the nuances of efforts to build communities at other sites, researchers may gain a better understanding of the ways communities form, develop, and are maintained. With further studies of teacher professional communities, researchers may gain a better understanding of the specifics of these teacher communities. By embracing the conflicts and the struggles rather than glossing over them, critics of teacher communities may better understand the benefits, drawbacks, and obstacles to communities, talking honestly about the dilemmas, the potential, and the pitfalls of communities in practice.

While this study explores the structures, processes, and development of two teacher professional communities, a similar framework could be used to study the relationship between in-school and out-of-school educational activities that build community, as well as the impact of community on the lives of students and teachers. For example, is it possible that when teachers work together to create a healthy school community, their own professional community is strengthened as well? While many reformers have attested to the connection between strong teacher and student/school communities, few have studied these interactions. Might teacher education be the best starting point for reshaping the culture of the school? What type of professional curriculum can best serve these interests?

Future Directions for Policymakers and Practitioners

The practical task of community-building in schools must follow the development of not only a clear conceptualization of community but also the specific values and commitments that such a conceptualization embodies and institutional structures that make those commitments real. Acknowledging and exploring the difficulties involved in such an undertaking is the first step toward creating and recreating schools in which teachers, administrators, and students engage in meaningful and communal relationships.

The complexities exposed by these case studies contribute to a growing understanding of the complexities practitioners and policymakers face in building teacher communities in schools. The evidence from Brandeis and Mills suggests that particular conditions for community that reform-minded policymakers and practitioners seek are necessary but insufficient. Specific participatory structures may break norms and expectations of privacy and these structures may have to be based on a clear and community-oriented vision. As Ann Lieberman writes, teachers must be "organized, mobilized [and] led" in order to overcome the norms of autonomy that pervade the school (Lieberman, 1988a).

Beliefs matter—not just that they are shared, but also that they embody commitments to ideals of community. For Brandeis, these ideals emphasized autonomy and responsibility; for Mills, different ideals include participation by all members of the community, equity, and inclusivity.[4]

Researchers, policymakers, and practitioners may need to acknowledge the relative differences in various beliefs about working together, working with students, and curricular aims and methods. Rather than fearing ideological commitments to one stance or another, school personnel would do well to recognize that different beliefs engender very different professional communities.

In "Reform or Reaction" Kantor and Lowe (1989) are critical of Grant's (1988) *The World We Created at Hamilton High* for just such reasons.

> Few can reasonably quarrel with Grant's desire for schools that will instill belief in a public purpose broader than the legal minimalism embodied in the defense of individual rights. But Grant fails to articulate in any but the most general terms the social basis on which that consensus might be built. (Kantor, 1989, p. 137)

Is one system of beliefs better than another? This very difficult question taken in its broadest sense is outside the scope of this book. However: Are certain beliefs more likely to result in participation by a diverse membership than others? Are certain beliefs more likely to inculcate a recognition of the importance of dissent in communal associations? Or the importance of equity among community members? Yes. Kantor (1989) continues:

> Any attempt to build a broader public purpose for American schooling must be based on an ethos that is rooted in the recognition of inequality of condition and that enlists the privileged in overcoming the disparities in opportunity. (p. 138)

Communities may need to pay particular attention to individual members, to opportunities for inclusion and interaction, and to a studied and thoughtful consideration of the dangers of insularity (Noddings, 1996).

The implications for schools are as follows: if teachers are to form professional communities in schools like Brandeis, it will be useful to acknowledge norms of professional autonomy and collegial—but independent—work. Participation and the expression of dissent would not be likely features of such professional communities.

---

4. The rhetoric of both communities, however, included participation, equity, and inclusivity.

If, on the other hand, reformers and practitioners prefer that teachers work in professional communities like the one found at Mills, teachers will need opportunities for common experiences that foster attachments, commitment, and participation. Bonds form between teachers as they work together toward common goals (McLaughlin & Talbert, 1993). Just as members of a close-knit drama group or political campaign develop attachments to each other and commitment to the group, teachers working in schools may need opportunities for interaction, mutual dependence, and identity. Building professional communities such as this one would mean "rendering more coherent those values that . . . uphold democratic participation and cooperation" (Kantor, 1989, p. 138).

Only by spending time among schoolteachers can school reformers and education researchers begin to understand and assist in their efforts. Further case studies would be beneficial to both researchers and policymakers to capture the real struggles of practitioners, committed to their profession and to each other, engaged in the work of building connections to one another and to their students. Researchers need stronger conceptualizations of the kinds of communities they are examining. Teachers and administrators need stronger visions of the type of community they are trying to build, whether it is communities based on some kind of professional autonomy or communities based on solidarity through a common mission. And policy analysts need the wherewithal to point out the differences and pursue strategies that truly represent a clear vision for communities in schools.

Methodology

This methodological appendix is devoted to the details of data collection, the progression of my own understandings through data analysis, and the personal predispositions that led to the findings and discussion presented to the reader.

DATA COLLECTION

The analytic and empirical work of this study draws from three sources. I examined the two teacher professional communities through (1) conceptions of teacher professional community stemming from the theoretical and philosophical literature on community and on the role of teacher community in educational reform; (2) empirical work (interviews) on teachers' disposition and beliefs about their workplace, specifically colleagueship, interaction, friendship, and school organization; and (3) empirical work (observations) on the qualities and features of teachers' professional relationships at the school site.

I employed two categories of populations in this study: *participating teachers and administrators* and a subpopulation of *target teachers*. The target teachers, who took part in more intensive interviews, were drawn from the group of participating teachers. Permission to recruit participants for the study was first obtained from the principal of each school.

I presented the study to *participating teachers* in the context of a meeting arranged initially by each principal. During this introductory group interview with teachers, I explained the purpose of the study, the methods to be used, and respondents' rights. I asked for the teachers' permission to conduct the research and solicited their cooperation. I had planned to interview only teachers who gave their voluntary, written consent. No teacher, however, declined to give written consent to be interviewed. During the preliminary interview I also asked for permission from four or five of the teachers in each school who are particularly interested in issues of teachers' workplace to be interviewed in greater depth and several times during the data collection period (*target teachers*). In all cases, I informed respondents that they could withdraw their consent at any time in accordance with the written consent forms.

Subjects' identities were kept confidential by assigning each an identification number and code name. These codes were used on all data forms and in any public reference to the subjects (such as conference presentations). Similarly, I assigned each school a pseudonym.

I conducted preliminary interviews with *participating teachers* to gain an overview of the organization, beliefs, and practices that comprise the school workplace and to identify potential target teachers for more in-depth interviews (interview protocols follow).

I conducted two hour-long interviews with *target teachers* and *administrators* to explore their understanding of specific events, beliefs, practices, norms, and behaviors that had contributed to the formation and maintenance of professional relationships at their school and, alternatively, events, beliefs, practices, norms, and behaviors that had impeded professional relationships. Additional half-hour, open-ended interviews took place after significant events during the data collection period.

I also interviewed target teachers and administrators to develop accounts of their ideal working environment and past professional or nonprofessional experiences they believe influenced their thinking about professional relationships.

In addition, I observed staff meetings, planning committees, staff development sessions, retreats, schoolwide educational events, and informal get-togethers among teachers during lunchtime, preparatory periods, and on field trips. I took written field notes and, at times, tape recorded the sessions (with the verbal permission of all those present).

Data collection also involved gathering of school- and district-level documents (planning strategies, brochures, newsletters, memos, meeting agendas) related to: (a) organization of the schools, (b) efforts to promote collegiality and a sense of community among the staff, and (c) plans for revamping the process by which school-based decisions are made. These documents and occasional interviews with administrators allowed me to corroborate findings and further refine earlier interpretations. In addition to observations within the school's printed schedule, data were collected before and after school, in between classes, and during other nonclass time (for example, teacher interviews before and after school).

The teachers' personal accounts and interviews helped to specify notions of teacher professional community held by teachers at each site. The observations, interviews, and audiotape analyses helped to clarify the nature of the teacher professional communities in each site. I asked teachers to reflect on my observations not only to test the accuracy of my statements but also to reexamine perceptions and conclusions, drawing on the insider knowledge of teachers, making them critics and interpreters.

After preliminary work in each school, I spent eight months shuttling between the two schools. My original intention was to go back and forth between the schools in one-month intervals. The intervals were quickly reduced to two and sometimes one week because of a need for greater continuity in observing school activities and following up key events with teacher interviews. Even the one-week pattern was sometimes broken for special events at either school. On many occasions, I attended weekend, evening, and holiday events in which teachers gathered for either professional or social reasons.

Although in each school I had obtained permission from participating teachers and the principal to attend any event unless otherwise advised, for any gathering outside of the routine, I asked for permission beforehand. In total, I was asked not to attend one meeting between four teachers in which one teacher's relationship to the others was under discussion because of worries about embarrassment during an already difficult discussion. I interviewed each of the participating teachers after this discussion.

I organized interviews by interviewee along the following categories: "educational, intellectual, and personal background," "preliminary," and "target teacher/administrator" interviews. Most interviews were taped and transcribed in full. In some, for the comfort of either myself or the interviewee, I took notes only and refrained from taping. In total, I conducted 28 interviews at Brandeis Middle School and 28 at C. Wright Mills Middle School.

I organized observations along the following categories: for Brandeis—"classroom observations," "sixth-grade department meetings," "other (organized) meetings," and "other"; for Mills—"classroom observations," "family faculty meetings," "full faculty meetings," "other (organized) meetings," and "other."

After the eight months of a near-constant presence was completed, I conducted sporadic visits the following two months to corroborate initial findings, share data with interviewees, and attend additional significant events (the closing of the school year and the final faculty meetings, for example).

ANALYSIS AND GROWING UNDERSTANDINGS

Data analysis took place throughout the data-collection year through a recursive process: cycling between refining strategies for data collection and thinking about the data I had already collected. The initial categories for sorting and coding the data reflected the features of community identified in Chapter 1. These were as follows:

1. Interaction and Participation
2. Interdependence
3. Shared Interests and Beliefs
4. Dissent
5. Meaningful Relationships

The following are among the individual factors affecting teaching community to which I gave attention:

1. Influential background experiences in other communities (positive or negative)
2. How individual teachers characterize their ideal workplace
3. Other significant aspects of their personal and professional lives (relationship status, age, dependents, personal projects, commitments, etc.)

4. Experiences in school of a particular teacher not indicative of the experiences of the majority of teachers studied)

In addition, I attended to the following organizational factors affecting teacher community:

1. School events determined by or occurring because of organizational features
2. School events undermined by organizational obstacles
3. Interpersonal and professional relationships structured/facilitated by the organization
4. Interpersonal and professional relationships undermined because of organization
5. Influence of a charismatic leader

I also looked for particular community-building experiences:

1. Explicitly community-building experiences (social gatherings, organized parties, "sunshine" funds, etc.) whose expressed goals were to have the faculty be more social
2. Subtle, inadvertent, circumstantial, and covert (known but hidden intentions by a leader) community-building experiences

Halfway through the study, I wrote a series of memos based on emerging categories. These memos allowed me to begin to examine in greater depth particular suspected patterns. I frequently added new categories when a new explanation or observation occurred to me and just as often let categories fall away for lack of sufficient evidence. The mid-year memos were as follows:

1. On a Climate/Culture of Participation
2. On Managing Difficult People and Difficult People Managing Themselves
3. On Community and Individuality—Not in Tension?
4. On Contrived (Artificial) and "Natural" Community-building Incidents
5. On Restructuring Efforts and Community-building
6. On Competition, Status, and Community
7. On a Shared Sense of Political Mission
8. On a Shared Sense of Pedagogical Mission
9. On Reinventing the Wheel
10. On Administration and Teacher Leadership (or the decline of the principal)
11. On Connections and Disconnections with Other Communities
12. On Attrition and Community Instability
13. On Cycles of Community Participation (e.g., whole-school to families to whole-school)
14. On Personalization vs. Favoritism (tyranny of the majority vs. tyranny of the popular or the eloquent)

For the remainder of the data collection and analysis, I revisited these memos, extending and explicating some, abandoning others, verifying some hunches, disproving others. These memos, distilled, eventually became the major foci of the study and led to the creation of the continuum described in Chapter 4 and the observations and conclusions in Chapter 5.

PERSONAL PREDISPOSITIONS

A ubiquitous poster advertisement for *Life* magazine a couple of years ago showed a picture of three children in a schoolyard, their teachers in the foreground, chatting and smiling. In plain view of the camera but apparently unbeknownst to the teachers, one child was carrying a gun neatly tucked into his trousers, the metallic butt glistening in the sunlight. The bottom of the poster sported the following caption: "We just take the pictures. You decide their meaning."

Nice slogan. Of course, it could not be further from the truth. The position from which the picture was taken, the type of lens used (telephoto or wide angle), even the editor's initial choice of setting, all strongly influence how the viewers "decide" the meaning. Similarly, in educational research, the researcher's choice of method, focus, scope, and research setting influence the resulting portrayal of findings.

As social scientists have shifted from claiming objectivity to questioning what objectivity might mean in different settings, a variety of new and rich methodologies have emerged as a result (Gitlin & Russell, 1994; Lather, 1991; Wolcott, 1994). The researcher's role and influence in conceptualizing a research problem, collecting data, distilling the data, and presenting findings have also increasingly become material for reflection and study. Moreover, the *choice* of method for conducting research is at long last subject to the kind of scrutiny once reserved only for the findings that resulted from such choices. In fact, the editors and photographers of *Life* magazine might concede, we take the pictures and, through choices made before, during, and after the picture-taking process, also nudge our audience on the path toward interpretation. While this would make for a duller slogan, it would be more honest.

Like the editors of *Life*, I too have personal predispositions. In this book, I have argued that Mills and Brandeis teachers function quite differently. The fact that both teacher professional communities can be adequately described by current rhetoric belies serious weaknesses in models for studying and building professional communities in schools. If the reader is eager to nurture and develop schools in which teachers are relatively autonomous, maintain a spectrum of views about education and the world, are supportive of one another, and both reflect and reinforce a more mainstream ideology of individual rights and freedoms, then Brandeis is a useful model of a well-functioning school in this regard. If, on the other hand, the reader is interested in schools that emphasize collective work and a collective mission around a stated and demonstrated commitment to critical thinking and implicit as well as explicit critiques of dominant ideologies, then the ways teachers conceive of and run Mills will be of interest.

As a researcher, I seek to demonstrate only that these two schools have dramatic differences and that the first step to moving from rhetoric to practice is to state clearly which type of professional community we hope to create and sustain. Furthermore, I have identified a spectrum along which Brandeis and Mills fall sometimes on one extreme, sometimes in the middle. Other schools will fall in different places and even require different spectra to describe them. For the purposes of this study, identifying the characteristics of community along a continuum of community ideals can help to clarify the motivations and dispositions of various types of teacher professional community.

As a practitioner and critic, however, I am partial to the mission of Mills faculty. I found the curriculum to be richer for the faculty's willingness to openly challenge students' thinking on a variety of ideologically dominant grounds, including but not limited to a strong democratic communitarian orientation. Of course, Brandeis has a strong ideology as well—one that is more consistent with the language of individual rights and responsibilities. The easy invisibility of Brandeis' ideology derives from its familiarity: Brandeis reflects the quest for autonomy and individualism so prevalent in our society.

My preferences, however, while certainly influencing the themes I chose to draw out, remained only preferences. In comparing the two schools, I sought to interrogate and clarify the underlying assumptions, motivations, and practices that give each teacher professional community its unique character.

References

Apple, M. W. (1987). Will the social context allow a tomorrow for tomorrow's teachers? *Teachers College Record, 88*(3), 330–337.

Arendt, H. (1972). *Crisis of the republic.* New York: Harcourt Brace Jovanovich.

Ashton, P., Doda, N., Webb, R. B., Olejnik, S., & McAuliffe, M. (1981). Middle school organization, teacher job satisfaction and school climate. In *Middle school research, selected studies 1981* (pp. 48–57). Fairborn, OH: National Middle School Association.

Bacharach, S. B., Bamberger, P., Conley, S. C., & Bauer, S. (1990). The dimensionality of decision participation in educational organizations: The value of a multi-domain evaluative approach. *Educational Administration Quarterly, 26,* 126–167.

Bacharach, S. B., Bauer, S. C., & Shedd, J. B. (1986). The work environment and school reform. *Teachers College Record, 88*(2), 241–256.

Barber, B. (1984). *Strong democracy: Participatory politics for a new age.* Berkeley: University of California Press.

Barth, R. S. (1988). Principals, teachers, and school leadership. *Phi Delta Kappan, 69*(9), 639–642.

Barth, R. S. (1990). *Improving schools from within: Teachers, parents, and principals can make a difference.* San Francisco: Jossey-Bass.

Bellah, R., Masden, R., Sullivan, W., Swidler, A., & Tipton, S. (1985). *Habits of the heart: Individualism and commitment in American life.* New York: Harper & Row.

Bettelheim, B. (1969). *The children of the dream.* New York: Macmillan.

Blasi, J. R. (1978). *The quality of life in a kibbutz cooperative community.* Cambridge, MA: Institute for Cooperative Community.

Blau, P. M., & Scott, W. R. (1962). *Formal organizations: A comparative approach.* San Francisco: Chandler Publishing Co.

Bloom, A. (1987). *The closing of the American mind.* New York: Simon and Schuster.

Bolman, L. G., & Deal, T. E. (1988). *Modern approaches to understanding and managing organizations.* San Francisco: Jossey-Bass.

Bourdieu, P. (1984). *Distinction: A social critique of the judgement of taste* (R. Nice, Trans.). Cambridge: Harvard University Press.

Bowman, R. F. (1984). Relationship educates: An interactive instructional strategy. *Contemporary Education, 55–56,* 103.

Boyer, E. (1990). *The condition of teaching: A state-by-state analysis.* Princeton, NJ: Carnegie Foundation for the Advancement of Teaching.

Brandeis, L. D. (1914/1933). *Business—a profession.* Boston: Hale, Cushman & Flint.

Brandeis, L. D. (1934). *The curse of bigness: Miscellaneous papers of Louis D. Brandeis*, (O. Fraenkel, Ed.). New York: Viking Press.

Bronfenbrenner, U. (1979). *The ecology of human development: Experiences by nature and design*. Cambridge, MA: Harvard University Press.

Bruffee, K. A. (1987). The art of collaborative learning: Making the most of knowledgeable peers. *Change, 19*(2), 42–47.

Bryan, C., & Erickson, E. (1970, June). *Structural effects on school behavior: A comparison of middle school and junior high school programs*. Grand Rapids, MI: Grand Rapids Public Schools.

Burbules, N. C., & Densmore, K. (1991). The limits of making teaching a profession. *Educational Policy, 5*(1), 44–63.

California State Department of Education, Middle Grade Task Force. (1987). *Caught in the middle: Educational reform for young adolescents in California public schools: Report of the Superintendent's middle grade task force*. Sacramento: California State Department of Education.

Carnegie Task Force on Teaching as a Profession. (1986). *A nation prepared: Teachers for the 21st century*. New York: Carnegie Corporation.

Cohen, D. K., McLaughlin, M. W., & Talbert, J. E. (Eds.). (1993). *Teaching for understanding: Challenges for policy and practice*. San Francisco: Jossey-Bass.

Cohen, E. G. (1994). *Designing groupwork* (2nd ed.). New York: Teachers College Press.

Coleman, J. S., Hoffer, T., & Kilgore, S. (1982). *High school achievement: Public, Catholic and private schools compared*. New York: Basic Books.

Conley, S. C. (1991). Review of research on teacher participation in school decision making. *Review of Research in Education, 17*, 225–266.

Counts, G. S. (1932). *Dare the school build a new social order*. New York: The John Day Company.

Cremin, L. A. (1988). *American education: The metropolitan experience, 1876–1980*. New York: Harper & Row.

Cuban, L. (1984). Transforming the frog into a prince: Effective schools research, policy, and practice at the district level. *Harvard Educational Review, 54*(2), 129–151.

Cuban, L. (1987). The Holmes Group report: Why reach exceeds grasp. *Teachers College Record, 88*(3), 348–353.

Darling-Hammond, L. (1988). Policy and professionalism. In A. Lieberman (Ed.), *Building a professional culture in schools* (pp. 55–77). New York: Teachers College Press.

Department of Education. (1991). *America 2000: An education strategy*. Washington, DC: U.S. Government Printing Office (ERIC Document Reproduction Service No. ED 327 009).

Dewey, J. (1916). *Democracy and education*. New York: Free Press.

Dewey, J. (1938). *Experience and education*. New York: Collier Books.

Dewey, J. (1956). *The child and the curriculum and The school and society*. Chicago: University of Chicago Press. (Original work published 1900)

Education Commission of the States. (1986). *What's next?: More leverage for teachers*. Denver: Education Commission of the States.

Eisner, E. (1984). The kind of schools we need. *Interchange, 15*(2), 1–12.

Eisner, E. (1998). *The enlightened eye: Qualitative inquiry and the enhancement of educational practice.* Upper Saddle River, NJ: Merrill.

Erikson, E. (1963). *Childhood and society* (2nd ed.). New York: Norton.

Etzioni, A. (1993). *The spirit of community: Rights, responsibilities, and the communitarian agenda.* New York: Crown Publishers.

Farges, B. (1993). *Project 2061 Learning Model.* San Francisco: California Office of Project 2061.

Feiman-Nemser, S., & Floden, R. E. (1986). The cultures of teaching. In M. C. Wittrock (Ed.), *Handbook of research on teaching* (3rd ed., pp. 505–526). New York: Macmillan.

Fine, D. R. (1986). *When leadership fails.* New Brunswick, NJ: Transaction Books.

Freire, P. (1970). *Pedagogy of the oppressed.* New York: Seabury Press.

Fromm, E. (1941). *Escape from freedom.* New York: Farrar and Rinehart.

Gardner, J. W. (1991). *Building community.* San Francisco: Independent Sector.

Geertz, C. (1973). *The interpretation of cultures.* New York: Basic Books.

George, P. (1983). *Theory Z school: Beyond effectiveness.* Columbus, OH: National Middle School Association.

Giroux, H. A. (1988). *Schooling and the struggle for public life: Critical pedagogy in the modern age.* Minneapolis: University of Minnesota Press.

Gitlin, A., & Russell, R. (1994). Alternative methodologies and the research context. In A. Gitlin (Ed.), *Power and method: Political activism and educational research* (pp. 181–202). New York: Routledge.

Goodlad, J. I. (1984). *A place called school: Prospects for the future.* New York: McGraw-Hill.

Goodlad, J. I. (1990). *Teachers for our nation's schools.* San Francisco: Jossey-Bass.

Goodman, N. (1978). *Ways of worldmaking.* Indianapolis, IN: Hackett Publishing Company.

Graham, P. (1967). *Progressive education: From arcady to academe.* New York: Teachers College Press.

Grant, G. (1988). *The world we created at Hamilton High.* Cambridge, MA: Harvard University Press.

Greely, A. M. (1975, Summer). On ethnicity and cultural pluralism. *Change, 7*(6) 4–7, 70–72.

Greene, M. (1985). The role of education in democracy [Special Issue]. *Educational Horizons, 63,* 3–9.

Greene, M. (1986). In search of critical pedagogy. *Harvard Educational Review, 56*(4), 427–440.

Greene, M. (1988). *Teaching and becoming a teacher.* Address at the Summer Institute for Teaching, Teachers College, New York.

Hannaway, J., & Talbert, J. (1993). Bringing context into effective schools research: Urban-suburban differences. *Educational Administration Quarterly, 29*(2), 164–186.

Hargreaves, A. (1990). *Individualism and individuality: Reinterpreting the teacher culture.* Paper presented at the annual meeting of the American Educational Research Association, Boston.

Hargreaves, A. (1994). *Changing teachers, changing times: Teachers' work and culture in the postmodern age*. London: Cassell.

Hillary, G. (1955). Definitions of community: Areas of agreement. *Rural Sociology* (20), 111–123.

Hirschi, T. (1969). *Causes of delinquency*. Berkeley: University of California Press.

Hoffer, E. (1951). *The true believer*. New York: Harper & Row.

Holmes Group. (1986). *Tomorrow's teachers: A report of the Holmes Group*. East Lansing, MI: Author.

hooks, b. (1994). *Outlaw culture: Resisting representations*. New York: Routledge.

Immegart, G. L. (1988). Leadership and leader behavior. In N. Boyan (Ed.), *Handbook of research on educational administration: A project of the American Educational Research Association* (pp. 259–277). New York: Longman.

Johnson, S. M. (1990). *Teachers at work: Achieving success in our schools*. New York: Basic Books.

Kantor, H. A., & Lowe, R. (1989). Reform or reaction. *Harvard Educational Review, 59*(1), 127–138.

Kidder, T. (1989). *Among schoolchildren*. Boston: Houghton Mifflin.

Kilpatrick, W. H. (1918). *The project method*. New York: Teachers College, Columbia University.

Kirst, M. W. (1984). *Who controls our schools? American values in conflict*. Stanford, CA: Stanford Alumni Association.

Kozol, J. (1972). *Free schools*. New York: Bantam Books.

Kruse, S. D., Louis, K. S., & Bryk, A. (1995). An emerging framework for analyzing school-based professional community. In K. S. Louis & S. D. Kruse (Eds.), *Professionalism and community: Perspectives on reforming urban schools* (pp. 23–44). Thousand Oaks, CA: Corwin.

Lampert, M. (1991, May). Looking at restructuring from within a restructured role. *Phi Delta Kappan, 72*(9), 670–674.

Lather, P. (1991). *Getting smart*. New York: Routledge.

Lieberman, A. (Ed.). (1986). *Rethinking school improvement: Research, craft, and concept*. New York: Teachers College Press.

Lieberman, A. (1987). Teacher leadership. *Teachers College Record, 88*(3), 400–405.

Lieberman, A. (Ed.). (1988a). *Building a professional culture in schools*. New York: Teachers College Press.

Lieberman, A. (1988b). Teachers and principals: Turf, tension, and new tasks. *Phi Delta Kappan, 69*(9), 648–653.

Lieberman, A. (1988c). Expanding the leadership team. *Educational Leadership, 45*(5), 4–8.

Lieberman, A. (1990). Teacher development in professional practice schools. *Teachers College Record, 92*(1), 105–122.

Lieberman, A. (1995). *The work of restructuring schools*. New York: Teachers College Press.

Lieberman, A., & Miller, L. (1984). *Teachers, their world, and their work*. Alexandria, VA: Association for Supervision and Curriculum Development.

Lightfoot, S. L. (1983). *The good high school*. New York: Basic Books.

Little, J. W. (1984). Seductive images and organizational realities in professional development. *Teachers College Record, 86*(1), 84–102.

Little, J. W. (1990). The persistence of privacy: Autonomy and initiative in teachers' professional relations. *Teachers College Record, 91*(4), 509–536.

Little, J. W., & McLaughlin, M. W. (1993). Introduction: Perspectives on cultures and contexts of teaching. In J. W. Little & M. W. McLaughlin (Eds.), *Teachers' work: Individuals, colleagues, and contexts.* New York: Teachers College Press.

Lortie, D. C. (1975). *Schoolteacher: A sociological study.* Chicago: University of Chicago Press.

Louis, K. S., & Kruse, S. D. (1995). *Professionalism and community: Perspectives on reforming urban schools.* Thousand Oaks, CA: Corwin.

Louis, K. S., Marks, H., & Kruse, S. D. (1994, April). *Teachers' professional community in restructuring schools.* Paper presented at the annual meeting of the American Educational Research Association, New Orleans, LA.

MacIntyre, A. (1981). *After virtue.* Notre Dame, IN: University of Notre Dame Press.

Maxwell, J. A. (1994, April). Diversity, solidarity, and community. Paper presented at the annual meeting of the American Educational Research Association, New Orleans.

McGee, J. C., & Blackburn, J. E. (1979). Administration of the middle school program. *Theory into Practice, 18*(1), 39–44.

McLaughlin, M. W. (1992, April). *Crafting community in secondary schools.* Address presented at the annual meeting of the American Educational Research Association, San Francisco.

McLaughlin, M. W. (1993). What matters most in teachers' workplace context? In J. W. Little & M. W. McLaughlin (Eds.), *Teachers' work: Individuals, colleagues, and contexts* (pp. 79–103). New York: Teachers College Press.

McLaughlin, M. W., & Talbert, J. (1993). Report of the center for research on secondary school contexts [presentation]. Stanford University.

McLaughlin, M. W., Talbert, J. E., & Bascia, N. (Eds.). (1990). *The contexts of teaching in secondary schools: Teachers' realities.* New York: Teachers College Press.

McLaughlin, M. W., Talbert, J., Kahne, J., & Powell, J. (1990, November). Constructing a personalized school environment. *Phi Delta Kappan, 72*(3), 230–235.

McLaughlin, M., & Yee, S. (1988). School as a place to have a career. In A. Lieberman (Ed.), *Building a professional culture in schools* (pp. 23–44). New York: Teachers College Press.

Meier, D. (1985). Retaining the teacher's perspective in the principalship. *Education and Urban Society, 17*(3), 302–310.

Meier, D. (1989, September 8). In education, small is sensible. *New York Times,* p. A16.

Meier, D. (1995). *The power of their ideas.* Boston: Beacon Press.

Merriam, S. B. (1988). *Case study research in education.* San Francisco: Jossey-Bass.

Merz, C., & Furman, G. (1997). *Community and schools: Promise and paradox.* New York: Teachers College Press.

Metz, M. H. (1986). *Different by design: The context and character of three magnet schools.* New York: Routledge & Kegan Paul.

Mills, C. W. (1963). *Power, politics & people: The collected essays of C. Wright Mills* (I. L. Horowitz, Ed.). New York: Oxford University Press.

National Commission on Excellence in Education. (1983). *A nation at risk: The imperative for educational reform.* Washington, DC: U.S. Department of Education.

Newmann, F. M., & Oliver, D. W. (1967). Education and community. *Harvard Educational Review, 37*(1), 61–106.

Newmann, F. M. (Ed.). (1994). Schoolwide professional communities. *Issues in Restructuring Schools* (Issue Report No. 6). Madison: Center on Organization and Restructuring of Schools, University of Wisconsin-Madison.

Nisbet, R. A. (1953). *The quest for community.* New York: Oxford University Press.

Noddings, N. (1988, February). An ethic of caring and its implications for instructional arrangements. *American Journal of Education,* pp. 215–230.

Noddings, N. (1992). *The challenge to care in schools: An alternative approach to education.* New York: Teachers College Press.

Noddings, N. (1996, Summer). On community. *Educational Theory, 46*(3), 245–267.

Perry, R. (1997). *The role of teachers' professional communities in the implementation of California mathematics reform.* Unpublished dissertation, Stanford University.

Peshkin, A. (1986). *God's choice: The total world of a fundamentalist Christian school.* Chicago: University of Chicago Press.

Pook, E. (1981). A study of the relationship of teacher job satisfaction and the level of implementation of recommended middle school practices. In *Middle school research: Selected studies 1981* (pp 1–9). Fairborn, OH: National Middle School Association.

Power, F. C., Higgins, A., & Kohlberg, L. (1989). *Lawrence Kohlberg's approach to moral education.* New York: Columbia University Press.

Rabinow, P. (Ed.). (1984). *The Foucault reader.* New York: Pantheon Books.

Ratzki, A. (1988). Creating a school community: One model of how it can be done. *American Educator, 12*(1), 38–43.

Rawls, J. (1971). *A theory of justice.* Cambridge, MA: Harvard University Press.

Raywid, M. A. (1984, October). *Preparing teachers for schools of choice.* Seminar Paper presented at a Hearing of the National Commission on Excellence in Teacher Education, Austin, TX.

Raywid, M. A. (1988). Community and schools: A prolegomenon. *Teachers College Record, 90*(2), 197–210.

Raywid, M. A. (1993). Community: An alternative school accomplishment. In G. A. Smith (Ed.), *Public schools that work: Creating community* (pp. 23–44). New York: Routledge.

Raywid, M. A. (1995). *Professional community and its yield at metro academy.* In K. S. Louis & S. D. Kruse (Eds.), *Professionalism and community: Perspectives on reforming urban schools* (pp. 45–75). Thousand Oaks, CA: Corwin.

Rosenholtz, S. J. (1989). *Teacher's workplace: The social organization of schools.* White Plains, NY: Longman.

Sandel, M. (1982). *Liberalism and the limits of justice.* Cambridge: Cambridge University Press.

Sarason, S. B. (1971). *The culture of the school and the problem of change.* Boston: Allyn and Bacon.

Scherer, J. (1972). *Contemporary community: Sociological illusion or reality?* London: Tavistock.

Selznick, P. (1992). *The moral commonwealth: Social theory and the promise of community.* Berkeley: University of California Press.

Sergiovanni, T. J. (1989). *Schooling for tomorrow: Directing reforms towards issues that count.* Boston: Allyn and Bacon.

Sergiovanni, T. J. (1994). *Building community in schools.* San Francisco: Jossey-Bass.

Shanker, A. (1987). Tomorrow's teachers. *Teachers College Record, 88*(3), 423–429.

Shulman, L. (1989). Teaching alone, learning together: Needed agendas for the new reforms. In T. Sergiovanni & J. Moore (Eds.), *Schooling for tomorrow: Directing reforms to issues that count* (pp. 166–187). Boston: Allyn and Bacon.

Sizer, T. R. (1984). *Horace's compromise: The dilemma of the American high school.* Boston: Houghton Mifflin.

Sizer, T. R. (1992). *Horace's school: Redesigning the American high school.* Boston: Houghton Mifflin.

Smylie, M. A. (1992). Teacher participation in school decision making: Assessing willingness to participate. *Educational Evaluation and Policy Analysis, 14*(1), 53–67.

Smylie, M. A., & Tuermer, U. (1995). Restructuring schools in Hammond, Indiana. In A. Lieberman (Ed.), *The work of restructuring schools: Building from the ground up* (pp. 87–110). New York: Teachers College Press.

Strike, K. A. (1991). The moral role of schooling in a liberal democratic society. In G. Grant (Ed.), *Review of research in education* (Vol. 17). Washington, DC: American Educational Research Association.

Talbert, J. (1993). Constructing a schoolwide professional community: The negotiated order of a performing arts school. In J. W. Little & M. W. McLaughlin (Eds.), *Teachers' work: Individuals, colleagues, and contexts* (pp. 164–184). New York: Teachers College Press.

Taylor, C. (1992). *Multiculturalism and the "politics of recognition."* Princeton: Princeton University Press.

Tillich, P. (1952). *The courage to be.* New Haven: Yale University Press.

Tocqueville, A. de. (1966). *Democracy in America* (G. Lawrence, Trans.). New York: Harper & Row.

Tönnies, F. (1887/1957). *Community and society (Gemeinschaft und Gesellschaft).* East Lansing: Michigan State University Press.

United States Bureau of the Census. (1996). Excerpted in Bayland Unified School District's annual district profile, 1995–96. Bayland, CA: Bayland Unified School District.

Varenne, H. (1983). *American school language: Culturally patterned conflicts in a suburban high school.* New York: Irvington Publishers.

Varenne, H. (1986). Part I: Telling America. In H. Varenne (Ed.), *Symbolizing America* (pp. 13–45). Lincoln: University of Nebraska Press.

Waller, W. W. (1932). *The sociology of teaching.* London: Chapman and Hall.

Walzer, M. (1983). *Spheres of justice.* New York: Basic Books.

Wehlage, G. G., Rutter, R. A., Smith, G. A., Lesko, N., & Fernandez, R. R. (1988). *Reducing the risk: Schools as communities of support.* London: Falmer Press.

West, C. (1990). The new cultural politics of difference. In R. Ferguson, M. Gever, T. Minh-ha, & C. West (Eds.), *Out there: Marginalization and contemporary cultures* (pp. 19–36). New York: The New Museum of Contemporary Art.

Westheimer, J. (1996). Essay review of *Building Community in Schools* by Thomas Sergiovanni. *Harvard Educational Review, 66*(4), 853–857.

Westheimer, J., & Kahne, J. (1993, December). Building school communities: An experience-based model. *Phi Delta Kappan, 75*(4), 324–328.

Westheimer, J., Kahne, J., & Gerstein, A. (1992). Reform for the nineties: Opportunities and obstacles for experiential educators. *Journal of Experiential Education, 15*(2), 44–49.

Wigginton, E. (1985). *Sometimes a shining moment: The Foxfire experience.* Garden City, NY: Anchor Press/Doubleday.

Wittrock, M. C. (Ed.). (1986). *Handbook of research on teaching* (3rd ed.). New York: Macmillan.

Wolcott, H. F. (1985). On ethnographic intent. *Educational Administration Quarterly, 21*(3), 187–203.

Wolcott, H. F. (1994). *Transforming qualitative data: Description, analysis, and interpretation.* Thousand Oaks, CA: Sage.

Zeichner, K. H. (1991). Contradictions and tensions in the professionalization of teaching and the democratization of schools. *Teachers College Record, 92*(3), 363–377.

Index

About the Author

Joel Westheimer is an assistant professor in the Department of Teaching and Learning and a Fellow in the Center for the Study of American Culture and Education at New York University. A former New York City Public Schools teacher, his articles on democratic education, service learning, and community have appeared in *Phi Delta Kappan, Harvard Educational Review, Curriculum Inquiry,* and the *Journal of Experiential Education,* among others. Recent awards include the New York University School of Education Griffiths Award for Educational Research and Cornell University's Jason Millman Promising Scholar Award, 1997. He lives in the East Village in New York City.